LEAN SIX SIGMA

YELLOW &
ORANGE BELT

MINDSET, SKILL SET AND TOOL SET

CLIMBING THE MOUNTAIN

ir. H.C. Theisens

FOURTH EDITION

Lean Six Sigma Academy©

Title:	Lean Six Sigma Yellow & Orange Belt Mindset, Skill set and Tool set
Series:	Climbing the Mountain
Author:	ir. H.C. Theisens
Co-authors:	D. Harborne
Graphics:	F. Hampsink, R. Verreijt
Publisher:	Lean Six Sigma Academy © Copyright LSSA BV, 2019 Amersfoort, the Netherlands
Contact:	Contact us or visit our website for more information, volume discounts, online sales and training material licensing www.lssa.eu info@lssa.eu

4th edition 2019
ISBN 978-94-92240-08-8
NUR 100

Printed in the Netherlands.

Content

Introduction

Would you consider to buy a new smart phone from a certain phone provider if your friends keep complaining about connection problems or bad service? You probably would not. You also would probably not want to go to a school with a reputation for poor teaching, a hospital with a high rate of infections due to bad hygiene or to eat in a restaurant that had served you bad food before. It does not matter what type of product or service we keep in mind; good service, good quality and a short response time are important for all products and services that we buy. For all types of products and services there is only one direction for response time, quality and price. We expect a product that meets our expectations and without any defect. Expected delivery time and response time should be shorter and quicker. The price we are willing to pay should be in line with the quality.

Because of the internet, consumers can obtain a huge amount of information about the performance of products and organizations. It is very easy to compare prices of different suppliers and ordering a product or service can be done at any time. If we want to buy a book, a jacket or even a car, we want to receive the product as soon as possible. On top of that we expect companies to develop new models every year. Of course we expect the price of a new model to be the same as the old model or even less.

Do you, as a consumer, have any idea what this means for companies that have to develop and deliver these products? In the past decades the increasing quality expectations and shorter Lead Times has had a huge impact on innovation, production, quality management and supply chain management. If a company is not able to keep up with this it will not survive. Each year many companies, both small and large, have to close their doors because they cannot meet the increasing expectations of customers. Companies and organizations must constantly improve their knowledge of processes and quality control in response to increase customer requirements for higher quality and shorter Lead Times.

Since process improvement has been going on for decades, process improvement techniques have been applied for decades. Different methods have been developed over the years like Lean Manufacturing, Kaizen, 'Theory of Constraints' (TOC), 'Total Quality Management' (TQM), 'Total Productive Maintenance' (TPM) and Six Sigma. Many books have been published about process improvement and quality management by people like Deming, Imai, Taiichi Ohno and Eliyahu Goldratt.

Different methods have helped different companies to make significant improvements. The approach that is most suitable for your organization depends very much on where it stands right now and what it needs to do in order to reach a higher level of performance. It is important to determine the level of operational excellence, before an improvement program is started. Over the past years an integration has taken place based on best practices from improvement methods like Kaizen, Lean, Six Sigma and others. This book will explain these different methods and an all-inclusive approach of the most commonly applied tools and techniques.

The road to the top of the mountain can be tough, as the path is full of technical and organizational obstacles. You will discover that the journey is also a very interesting, instructive and satisfactory one. The roadmap and techniques described in this book will give insight and understanding of a number of powerful tools and techniques to improve processes and quality.

How to use this book

Thousands of books have been published over the years about process improvement and quality management. You can find many different books on the topics Lean Management and Six Sigma. This book is different because it reviews an approach across all improvement methods that have been proven to be successful over the past decades, such as TQM, Kaizen, TPM, Lean and Six Sigma. These methods, tools and techniques have been united in the 'Continuous Improvement Maturity Model' (CIMM™). This is a framework describes the process of continuous improvement from a very early stage through delivering World Class products and services. The CIMM framework connects Lean, Six Sigma and other improvement methods. The framework incorporates the best practices methods and techniques of process improvement, quality management and new product development. CIMM is an open standard and is maintained by the 'Lean Six Sigma Academy' (LSSA).

The structure of this book is based on the Lean Six Sigma Academy Syllabi for Yellow Belt [6.] and Orange Belt [7.]. All of the techniques described in these Syllabi will be reviewed in this book. We also advise you to use the accompanying 'Lean Six Sigma Yellow Belt & Orange Belt Exercise book' (ISBN 978-94-92240-05-7). Information about the Lean Six Sigma certification process is reviewed in Appendix A. We advise you to register this book at www.lssa.eu. After registering you will be able to download additional examples and templates.

Those who would like to apply Lean Six Sigma at the Green or Black Belt level are advised to read the 'Lean Six Sigma Green Belt' book or 'Lean Six Sigma Black Belt' book and the accompanying exercise book from the series 'Climbing the Mountain'.

As the entire journey of becoming World Class cannot be taken overnight, you do not have to read this book entirely at once. We recommend to start reading the first three chapters. It will give insight into the five CIMM levels and at what level your organization is currently acting. This will clarify which chapters will be interesting for you to read and which techniques useful to apply. The CIMM framework will guide you to define the most appropriate approach for the situation your organization is currently in. Guidelines are given that will help you and your organization from the very beginning till World Class performance. I wish you the best of luck on your journey of 'Climbing the Mountain'.

To aid readability this book has been written with male gender pronouns, but in every case a female gender pronoun could equally be substituted.

Preface

What would it be like to work in an organization where everything is predictable and runs smoothly? How would it be if you as a quality employee or process owner no longer have to deal with errors or incidents? How would it be for a manager if the strategy is clear, everyone knows what his or her contribution is and there is enough time for all projects? Unfortunately, reality is very different for most organizations. Even though organizations often look beautiful from the outside, there is still a lot to improve and processes are not nearly as stable and predictable as you would like.

Many organizations currently apply Lean Six Sigma as a holistic approach for process improvement. This approach is supplemented with principles and techniques from other improvement methods such as Total Productive Maintenance (TPM), Business Process Management (BPM) and Theory of Constraints (TOC). It is precisely the combination of the different methodologies that helps organizations best.

It is important to realize that applying improvement techniques is only one side of the story. What is at least as important is the creation of a continuous improvement culture. This covers matters such as strategy, leadership, organizational structure, change management and team development. This is also referred to as the 'soft' side of process improvement, but in practice this is often the most difficult aspect. It is necessary to make people work in a different way. However, changing the organization is not easy. People in general do not like change, unless they see the benefit of the change. Implementing an operational excellence successfully is a major challenge for management. I hope that this book will serve as a guideline for selecting the right projects, successfully executing these projects and to lead change.

I want to thank everyone who helped with reviewing this book. In total, around 25 experts from various companies and organizations made a valuable contribution. I would also like to thank the people who have contributed to the development of the 'Continuous Improvement Maturity Model' that has already helped many organizations in determining their improvement strategy. This model has been the basis for this book.

ir. H.C. Theisens
Master Black Belt Symbol B.V. (the Netherlands)

"It always seems impossible,

until its done."

- Nelson Mandela -

1
World Class Performance

1

World Class Performance is the highest level that a company can reach within its own sector by developing new products and services that exceed customer expectation in a very short time-to-market. In order to achieve World Class Performance, organizations need to develop and produce products and services that are the best in the world. Its production and delivery process should perform at the level of Operational Excellence and the organization should continuously improve its processes. The organization needs to be innovative, agile and should have a high ability for renewal.

World Class Performance is not something that you can realize in a few months. There is no golden roadmap to success. Working to become World Class is a long and bumpy journey with successes and setbacks. There will be roadblocks on the winding way to the top of the mountain. It is very unlikely that all people involved will reach the summit. Some will fall behind. Others will drop off completely. Although this is not a joyful perspective, it is a path that must be followed if you want to stay competitive in the future as most of your competitors work on Continuous Improvement.

1.1 Competitive strategies

Each company has the same challenge: 'How can we provide products or services with maximum value for our clients at the lowest possible costs and with the shortest delivery time?' Michael Treacy and Fred Wiersema described in there book 'The Discipline of Market Leaders' (1997), three generic competitive strategies: Operational Excellence, Customer Intimacy and Product Leadership. According to the authors a company should embrace and become successful in at least one of these three strategies, and perform to an acceptable level in the other two.

1.1.1 Operational Excellence

Continuous improvement methods like Lean and Six Sigma support organization to become successful in 'Operational Excellence'. Operational Excellence focuses on delivering to customer expectation, without failures, on time and in a cost-efficient manner. It is a philosophy where problem solving, teamwork and leadership result in the on-going improvement of the organization. Operational Excellence involves focusing on the customer's needs, keeping the employees positive and empowered and continually improving the current activities in the workplace. This strategy is often followed by high-volume and transaction-oriented companies that operate in a mature and commoditized market.

1.1.2 Physical versus Transactional processes

In general, processes can be divided into two groups. The first group is physical processes. The second group is transactional processes. Most companies tend to have both types of processes, but have a focus on one of these groups. In Table 1.1 a number of examples are listed for both groups.

Although Lean Six Sigma finds its origin in manufacturing, it is often applied within service organizations as well. It is good to realize some of the similarities and differences between physical processes and transactional processes:

- Transactional environments tend to have a stronger need for fast adaptability as customers' requirements change more frequently.
- Inventory is less visible in transactional environments, as most work in process has the form of electronic data and correspondence rather than physical items.
- Transactions within one process take place on computer systems that are connected across multiple locations, sometimes around the world, while manufacturing processes are more centralized in one location.
- The connection of different manufacturing processes is much more complicated as parts are produced around the world by different companies, making it a logistical challenge to get all parts together at the right moment without huge piles of inventories.
- Maintenance has a different meaning within transactional environments, as computer software and algorithms do not wear out like equipment and tooling.
- Transactional processes tend to have more waiting time than manufacturing. In most cases this is the consequence of several approval steps in the process.
- Transactional processes are less data-driven. Even if data is recorded, it is hidden in systems. People are unaware or do not have access to data or do not look for data to support decisions. As a consequence decisions are often based on opinions rather than facts.
- People in service organizations tend to have less affinity with statistical analysis, whereas this is an important element within Six Sigma.

If you read all the above, you might think that Lean Six Sigma is difficult to apply in service organizations. This is not the case, although it requires a different approach. On the other hand, transactional processes have great opportunities for improvement, as there is more low-hanging fruit and more waiting time.

Table 1.1. *Overview of processes*

Sector	Process type
Physical processes (Manufacturing)	Assembling, connecting
	Forming, machining
	Chemical processing
	Joining, finishing
	Testing (e.g. inspection, electrical, laboratories)
	Groceries, shops, restaurants, etc.
	Distribution, transportation & logistics
	Construction
Transactional processes (Service)	Strategic planning process
	New product development & IT development
	Financial transactions
	(e.g. billing, invoicing, banking, insurance)
	Request for quotation
	Customer service
	Complaint management
	Planning process & order entry process
	Human resource management

1.2 History of Continuous Improvement

1

In the last few years, the Lean and the Six Sigma philosophies have merged to Lean Six Sigma as a complete approach for process improvement. It is a combination of Lean Manufacturing and Six Sigma and uses a combined set of tools that can be applied to reduce Lead Time, reduce operational cost and improve quality. This will provides organizations with greater speed, less variation and more bottom-line impact.

1.2.1 History of Total Quality Management, Lean and Six Sigma

In this section we will review the history of quality management in general and Lean Manufacturing and Six Sigma in particular.

History of Quality Management

The origin of managing quality goes back thousands of years. Building the great pyramids of Cheops in 2560 BC could not have been done without proper quality management. Even today we are astonished by the way the 5.5 million tons of limestone, 8,000 tons of granite and 500,000 tons of mortar were used in the construction of the Great Pyramid. The largest granite stones in the pyramid weigh 25 to 80 tons. The accuracy of the pyramids workmanship is such that the four sides of the base have an average error of only 58 millimeters in length. The base is horizontal and flat to within ±15 mm. These numbers prove that the level of quality was very high.

The concept of quality as we think of it now first emerged during the industrial revolution. Previously, goods had been made from start to finish by the same person or team of people, with handcrafting and tweaking the product to meet quality criteria. Mass production brought huge teams of people together to work on specific stages of production where one person would not necessarily complete a product from start to finish. In the late 19th century pioneers such as Taylor and Henry Ford recognized the limitations of the methods being used in mass production at the time and the varying quality of output. Henry Ford (1863 - 1947) was the founder of Ford Motor Company and sponsor of the development of the assembly line technique of mass production. Many would say that Lean started with Henry Ford. Initially this was more a Lean initiative than a quality management initiative. Each T-Ford was supplied in any desired color, as long as it was black, and it was supplied with a tool box in the trunk. Later Ford emphasized standardization of design and component standards to ensure a standard product was produced. Management of quality was the responsibility of the Quality department and was implemented by inspection of product output to catch defects.

Shewhart (1891 - 1967) was an American physicist, and known as the father of statistical quality control. He has set the basis for the Control chart and bringing the production process into a state of Statistical Process Control (SPC). He is also the creator of the PDCA circle. The application of statistical control evolved during World War II where quality became a critical component of the war effort.

After World War II the Japanese welcomed the input of Americans Juran (1904 - 2008) and Deming (1900 - 1993). Juran was a management consultant and engineer. He wrote several influential books on quality management. He was one of the first to write about the 'Cost of Poor Quality' (COPQ). He is also known for the Pareto tool or '80/20 rule'. Deming was a statistician after whom the Deming Prize for quality is named (1951). Deming proclaimed the PDCA circle for solving problems from Shewhart. Deming is regarded as having had more impact upon Japanese manufacturing and business than any other individual of Japanese heritage. He was only just beginning to win widespread recognition in the U.S. at the time of his death in 1993.

Masaaki Imai (born 1930) is a Japanese organizational theorist and management consultant, known for his work on quality management, specifically on Kaizen. In 1986 he founded the Kaizen Institute to help Western companies introducing the concepts, systems and tools of Kaizen.

1

'Total Quality Management' (TQM) in the United States came much later as a direct response to the quality revolution in Japan. By the 1970s, U.S. industrial sectors such as automobiles and electronics had been broadsided by Japan's high-quality competition. The U.S. response became known as 'Total Quality Management' and consists of continuously improving the ability to deliver high-quality products and services to customers. TQM typically relies heavily on the previously developed tools and techniques of quality control. TQM enjoyed widespread attention during the late 1980s and early 1990s before being overshadowed by ISO 9001, Lean Manufacturing and Six Sigma. Many of its principles and tools however are still present in today's quality management programs.

History of Lean Manufacturing

Lean Manufacturing focuses on stability and elimination of waste. Lean Manufacturing began with Henry Ford who was the first person to truly integrate an entire production process. He did this by lining up fabrication steps in process sequence using Standardized Work and interchangeable parts. Ford called this 'Flow' production (1913). The problem with Ford's system was its inability to provide variety. As mentioned the Model-T was limited to one color and to one specification. As a result, all Model-T chassis were essentially identical until the end of production in 1926.

In the 1930s, and more intensely just after World War II (1950), Kiichiro Toyoda, Taiichi Ohno, and others at Toyota started looking at Ford's situation. While Ford was producing 8,000 vehicles per day, Toyota had produced only 2,500 vehicles in 13 years. Toyota wanted to scale up production but lacked the financial resources required for the huge quantity of inventory and subassemblies as seen at the Ford's plant. It occurred to them that a series of simple innovations might make it possible to provide both continuity in process flow as well as a wide variety of product offerings. Soon after, Toyota developed the 'Toyota Production System' (TPS). TPS borrowed ideas from Ford but developed the 'Just In Time' philosophy (JIT), the 'Pull Concept' and 'Jidoka' to address the issues of high cost associated with Ford's large inventories. The Lean thought process is thoroughly described in the book 'The machine that changed the World' (Womack and Jones, 1990) and in a subsequent volume, 'Lean Thinking' (1996), which specifically describes the five Lean principles [see section 6].

In 2008 Toyota became the world's largest auto manufacturer in terms of overall sales. Over the past two decades, Toyota's continued success has created an enormous demand for further knowledge concerning Lean Thinking. There are literally hundreds of books, papers and other resources currently available to this growing Lean Management audience.

Lean Thinking or Lean Management has been widely distributed around the world. Lean principles and tools are being used in production, logistics and distribution, services, trade, health, construction, maintenance and even in government with the common goal of reducing turnaround time and operational costs while at the same time improving quality. One of the most important activities within Lean programs is the identification and elimination of Waste or Muda.

History of Six Sigma

It was 1979 when Motorola was engaged in a painful process of self-discovery and began to realize the extent to which it had lost market share in many key segments, including televisions, car radios and semiconductors. That same year, during a company officers' meeting, Motorola's President and CEO Bob Galvin asked the question, 'What is wrong with our company?' Many officers and corporate chiefs began voicing the standard, politically correct excuses. Blame it on the Japanese, blame it on the economy in general, blame it on weak research and development.

While all this was going on, a lone voice in the back of the room spoke up loudly and clearly saying 'I will tell you what is wrong with this company... our quality stinks!' That voice was Art Sundry, a sales manager for Motorola's most profitable business at the time. Everyone thought he would be fired for this ballsy assertion. How could someone make such a statement in such horrible and turbulent times? Surely Motorola had always been and still was among the world's best manufacturers, regardless of the hard times it was facing. (Mikel J. Harry, www.mikeljharry.com).

Motorola was at a major turning point in its history. It could continue on a downward trend relative to competitors, or it could break that trend with an ambitious culture change and quality improvement initiative. This was the moment Motorola began its search for ways to eliminate waste and improve its quality. Two Motorola engineers, Bill Smith and Mikel Harry, were credited for their pioneering work aimed at improving processes and for finding and resolving defects. Their work on process capability, tolerance, critical-to-quality characteristics, and design margins laid much of the foundation for what today is called Six Sigma.

Six Sigma focuses on capability and reducing variation. Recognizing a link between fewer defects and lower costs, Motorola set out to incorporate this connection into their manufacturing processes, which they called 'Six Sigma'. Motorola's Six Sigma quality program was so radical that managers were forced to think about the business differently. Applying these concepts to Motorola's electronics manufacturing delivered more than $2.2 billion in benefits within four years and $16 billion within 15 years. Motorola's CEO Bob Galvin cited the work of Bill Smith and Mikel Harry in achieving these benefits.

One of the companies that embraced the Six Sigma philosophy was General Electric (GE). GE Chairman, Jack Welch was told that Six Sigma could have a profound effect on GE's quality. Although skeptical at first, Welch initiated a huge campaign called 'the GE Way'. He made an official announcement and launched the quality initiative at GE's annual gathering of 500 top managers in January 1996. Welch described the program as 'The biggest opportunity for growth, increased profitability, and individual employee satisfaction in the history of the company'. His goal was to take quality to a whole new level and to become a Six Sigma quality company, producing nearly defect-free products and providing nearly defect-free services and transactions. Welch's intention was to infuse quality into every corner of the company. He later called Six Sigma 'the most difficult stretch goal', but also suggested that it was 'The most important initiative GE had ever undertaken'. General Electric saved more than $12 billion with Six Sigma in the five years after implementation.

1.3 Philosophy and principles

The aspect 'Philosophy & Principles' explains the values and principles of Lean and Six Sigma. In this section the principles of Toyota and the House of Quality will be reviewed.

1

1.3.1 Value and foundations of Lean and Six Sigma
Both Lean and Six Sigma have a strong foundation of improving customer value. Far from meaning we should ignore the needs and values of the organization in favor of those of the customer. Instead this leads us to develop a thorough understanding of how improving customer values will aid the objectives of the organization. This provides a powerful win-win sense of purpose that helps guide every improvement decision made.

Lean Six Sigma comprises a set of powerful tools and techniques that will help any organization to improve its efficiency and effectiveness. Classically, Lean is often presented as the approach to use to achieve improved efficiency and process velocity through the 'relentless pursuit of the elimination of Waste', and Six Sigma is presented as the approach to use to achieve improved effectiveness and process quality by reducing variation. However, a closer look shows that Lean contains a key pillar of 'building in quality' and Six Sigma can be used to understand where variation is the root cause of failures to achieve process lead times. It is more useful to consider the current maturity of an organization's system of process improvement when considering whether to apply Lean or Six Sigma tools and techniques. We will see later a model that, for the first time, helps us to do exactly this.

1.3.2 Lean principles
Womack, Jones and Roos published two successful books entitled 'The machine that changed the World' (1990) and 'Lean Thinking' (1996) [8.]. Both books address the revolution in manufacturing represented by the Toyota Production System of the Toyota Corporation of Japan. They compared this way of working with the traditional mass production system that was used by other companies in the Western world. They described in their book 'Lean Thinking' the following five principles:

Table 1.2. *Lean principles*

Lean principle	Description
Value	Define what is of value to the customer
Value Stream	Identify the value stream / eliminate waste
Flow	Create a constant flow
Pull	Produce based on demand
Perfection	Continuous improvement

In paragraph 6 we will review each of these five principles in more detail and also show how applying these principles will result in shorter lead times and better quality.

1

Toyota developed the 'Toyota Production System' (TPS). TPS borrowed ideas from Ford but developed the 'Just In Time' philosophy (JIT) and the 'Pull Concept' to address the issues of high cost associated with Ford's large inventories. The Toyota Production System is an integrated system that comprises its management philosophy and practices. A detailed description of the system and its 14 principles are described in the book 'The Toyota Way' (Jeffrey K. Liker, PhD, 2004) [4.].

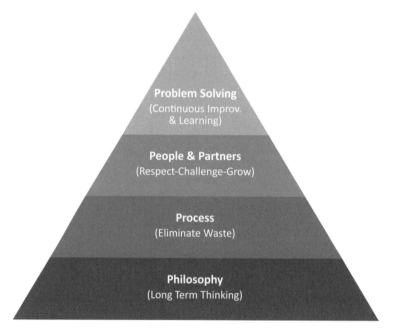

Figure 1 - *Toyota Production System (Liker, 2004)*

Philosophy:
1. Base your management decisions on a long-term philosophy, even at the expense of short-term financial goals.

Process:
2. Create a process flow to surface problems.
3. Use Pull systems to avoid overproduction.
4. Level out the workload (Heijunka).
5. Stop when there is a quality problem (Jidoka).
6. Standardize tasks for Continuous Improvement.
7. Use visual control so no problems are hidden.
8. Use only reliable, thoroughly tested technology.

People & Partners:
9. Create leaders who live the philosophy.
10. Respect, develop and challenge your people and teams.
11. Respect, challenge and help your suppliers.

Problem Solving:
12. Go see for yourself to thoroughly understand the situation.
13. Make decisions slowly by consensus, thoroughly considering all options; implement decisions rapidly.
14. Become a learning organization through relentless reflection (Hansei) and Continuous Improvement (Kaizen).

Toyota visualized its values, principles, way of working and the most important tools in the Toyota House of Quality. The roof of the house expresses the goals of the organization (Best Quality - Lowest Cost - Shortest Lead Time - Best Safety - High Morale). The foundation of the house addresses the principles, followed by a number of conditions that are always needed. Here you can find Standardized Work and Visual management. There are two pillars. The first pillar is called Jidoka and is about 'Building in quality'. The second pillar is called 'Just In Time' and includes a number of logistical principles and tools. The center of the House visualizes the continuous effort of improving the organization. This includes the crucial element 'People and Teamwork'. To become a Lean thinking company one has to change permanently the attitude and behavior of its management and employees. Many of the techniques listed in this House of Quality will be reviewed in this book.

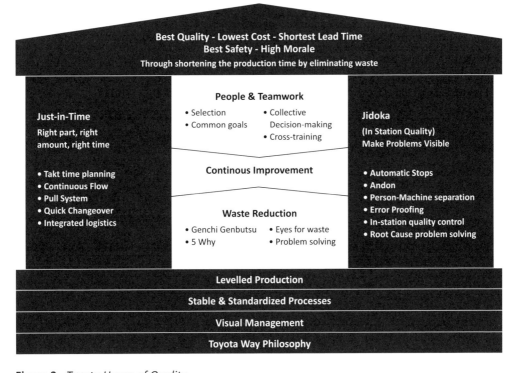

Figure 2 - *Toyota House of Quality*

1.3.3 Six Sigma principles

Six Sigma is a long-term, forward-thinking initiative designed to fundamentally change the way corporations do business. It is first and foremost a 'Business improvement method' that enables companies to increase profits by streamlining operations, improving quality and eliminating defects or mistakes in everything a company does. While traditional quality programs have focused on detecting and correcting defects, Six Sigma encompasses something broader. It provides specific methods to recreate the process so that defects are significantly reduced or even completely prevented [2.].

'Critical to Quality' measures (CTQs) are the key characteristics of a product or process which performance standards or specification limits must meet in order to satisfy the customer. CTQs can be measured and its data can be analyzed. A measurement that falls outside the CTQ specification limits is called a defect. A 'defect' in a product does not necessarily mean that the product is damaged or broken, but that the CTQ is outside its specification. Products that perform outside the specification, can still be functional. The objective of Six Sigma is to reduce the variation of the CTQ values by identifying and removing its causes of variations. This can be done in both manufacturing and business processes.

The maturity of a process can be described by a Sigma rating, indicating the yield or percentage of defect-free products it creates. A process performing at a Six Sigma level means that 99.99966% of the products produced are within specification. Processes that perform at the 'level of 6 Sigma' are assumed to produce less than 3.4 defects per million opportunities (DPMO). Six Sigma's implicit goal is to improve a process, but not with the intention that in all cases the above mentioned level of 6 sigma (eq. to 3.4 DPMO) should be achieved. Actually, the Six Sigma philosophy is to realize breakthroughs in quality performance.

Six Sigma is more sophisticated than applying simple problem solving tools. Six Sigma applies statistical tools to identify and remove causes of variation for which measures are needed. For applying statistical tools you need to keep in mind the statistical fundamental rules. Most noteworthy is that you have to be very careful how you apply statistical tools when the set of data represents an instable process. For instance, it is not allowed to apply a normal distribution analysis on a set of data that contains outliers from an instable process or measurement. The first step in a breakthrough process should always be to investigate the stability of the data set and the process performance over time. The Six Sigma toolbox contains a number of tools that can be applied to visualize and analyze the stability performance of a process. When the defects are mainly caused by an instable process, the process of searching for its root causes is more likely to involve the application of basic problem solving tools. A proper maintenance program or a Lean or Kaizen approach should be applied in order to remove the cause for the instability before continuing with a variation reduction initiative with sophisticated Six Sigma tools.

1.4 Organizational process management

Each organization has the same challenge: "How can we provide products and services with maximum value for our customers, at the lowest possible cost and with the shortest delivery time?" Even if an organization still develops such beautiful products or provides the best services, it is necessary that these are delivered without errors, efficient and predictable.

In order to achieve this, organizations must constantly work to improve their processes and develop the organization. Continuous improvement consists of both visible and invisible aspects. The visible aspects are the techniques and activities, while the invisible aspects are the strategy, leadership, competencies and involvement of the employees. It is not just about improving the processes, but continuous improvement must also focus on developing the organization and its employees.

1.4.1 Continuous Improvement Maturity Model
To support organizations in the continuous improvement process, the LSSA has developed the 'Continuous Improvement Maturity Model' (CIMMTM). CIMM summarizes all best practices elements of many different improvement methods in one framework. The model is build up of three areas of importance:

- PEOPLE   Employees who carry out the activities.
- PROCESS   Coherence of activities that result in a product or service.
- PRODUCT   The product or service as well as the tools and systems required for delivery.

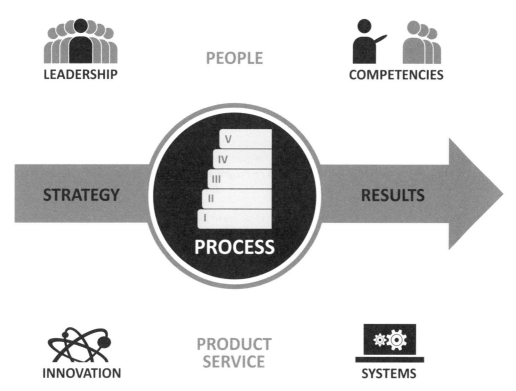

Figure 3 - *Business Improvement Model (LSSA, 2014)*

1

These three areas are interlinked with each other. A change in one of these areas will affect the other two. A change in the process for example, will affect the work of staff. Employees will probably need to get new instructions or be trained to work in this new way. Introducing a new product or service will require new equipment, new tools or a change in the information system. It is therefore of paramount importance that each element receives proper attention before and during a change in each other element in order to prevent quality or delivery issues.

Let's take a closer look at the 'Process'-section. Improving processes within the organization is described in more detail in Figure 4. An approach is described of process improvement from creating a solid foundation to developing future-proof processes. CIMM incorporates the best practices, methods and techniques of process improvement, quality management and new product development. It includes elements from TQM, Kaizen, TPM, Lean, Six Sigma and Design for Six Sigma.

1. Creating a solid foundation (Structured) - [see Chapter 4]:
    Before organizations can work on process improvement programs like Lean and Six Sigma, it is necessary to establish a proper foundation. The basic principle of the first level includes a safe and professional work environment, reliable equipment and standardized work (clear procedures, work instructions and protocols). This provides a solid foundation for all future initiatives and improvement programs. At this level, we are working to create a safe and organized work environment, standardized work and a quality management system.

2. Creating a Continuous Improvement culture (Managed) - [See Chapter 5]:
    The second level focuses on creating a culture in which all employees are involved in the improvement process. This level follows the Kaizen philosophy of Masaaki Imai. Kaizen focuses on improvements in the workplace, in Japanese called the 'Gemba'. The Kaizen philosophy is based on a process of continuous improvement in small steps. The idea behind this is that by realizing a large number of minor improvements, eventually a big improvement has been achieved. Also, it is much easier for employees to adapt to small changes instead of dealing with a major change. The process improvement roadmap used at this level is the PDCA cycle, which stands for Plan - Do - Check - Act. A Kaizen project lasts about a few days and is often executed by employees at the shop floor. In order to support the realization of a continuous improvement culture, it is important to involve as many employees as possible so that the entire team becomes part of the improvement culture. Communication about daily performance is important to keep everyone involved and to keep track of daily performance. This is achieved through the introduction of communication boards. Short stand-up meetings may be organized daily to review daily performance, address issues and to assign actions to be taken.

3. Create stable and predictable processes (Predictable) - [see Chapter 6]:
    The third level focuses on creating stable and reliable processes with a predictable outcome. The main goal of creating predictable processes is the prevention of unsafe situations, stress, firefighting, long delivery times and poor quality. In other words, creating an environment where one knows what will happen and where clear promises can be made to customers. Remember that a reliable delivery time is usually better than a fast but unreliable delivery time. This level focuses primary on optimizing operational logistics rather than quality improvement. However, by creating stable and reliable processes, where people focus solely on adding value and eliminating waste, the quality also automatically increases. The five Lean principles are the basis for this level. Processes are described and deployed in an efficient manner by identifying and eliminating wastes.

4. Create capable processes (Capable) - [See Chapter 7]:
   The fourth level focuses on reducing the variation of the stable processes created in the first three levels. The goal is to increase predictability and quality. The improvement method used in this level is Six Sigma. Six Sigma's starting principle is reducing variation and increase capability. The roadmap followed at this level is the DMAIC approach, which stands for Define - Measure - Analyze - Improve - Control. At this stage, Green and Black Belts apply statistical techniques to analyze and improve the performance of processes and products. This approach is suitable for problems that cannot be solved by applying simple techniques. A Six Sigma project usually takes 3 to 6 months and is led by a Green or Black Belt, supported by Yellow and Orange Belts.

5. Create future-proof processes (Sustained) [See Chapter 8]:
   The fifth level is a combination of 'Product Lifecycle Management' (PLM) and 'Design for Six Sigma' (DfSS). PLM is the process of controlling the entire product lifecycle (development, growth, maturity, decline). DfSS is a systematic approach and application of some powerful techniques in the development process of new products or systems. The goal of DfSS is to ensure that new products are performing at a high quality level from the first day of production. DfSS brings the process much more into a controlled state by focusing on risks and on critical customer requirements from the first stage of the development process. The application of Design for Six Sigma is done by Black Belts, Reliability Engineers and, in some cases, by Green Belts. This level therefore falls outside the scope of this book. We will only briefly discuss the DMADV roadmap that is used in DfSS.

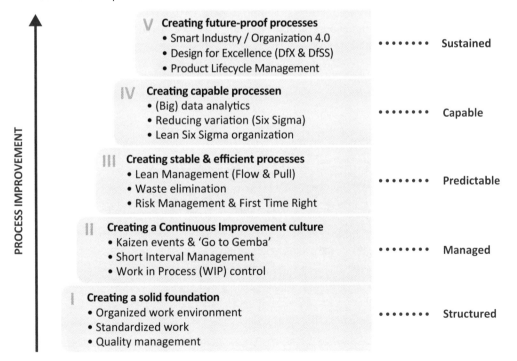

Figure 4 - *CIMM Process Improvement*

1.5 Project selection process

Every organization continuously works on all kinds of different projects, like new business opportunities, new product development, installing equipment, system implementation, Continuous Improvement projects, cost reduction programs, organizational changes etc. There are large projects that take months and small projects that only take days. In addition there are projects with a high risk of failure and there are projects with low risk. Furthermore there are 'Low-hanging fruit' projects and there are complex projects that need to be staffed by engineers and Black Belts. Resources however are limited, so choices have to be made. In this section we will review several techniques that can support to make these choices.

1.5.1 Financial measures

Despite the type of customer complaint or request, in the end it is all about 'Costs'. Even if the issue is about quality or delivery, it can be converted to costs. For the management to make decisions about prioritizing projects, the problem statement should be converted to 'Costs', as Philip Crosby stated in his book 'Quality is Free' (1979): "Money is the language of management; you need to show them the numbers". In this section we will review the definition of 'Costs of Poor Quality' (CoPQ).

Costs can be separated into visible and invisible costs. Visible CoPQ are easy to identify and easily measured, while invisible CoPQ are difficult to identify and not easy to measure. The combination of visible and invisible CoPQ are represented as an iceberg. Only a small amount of the costs is visible, represented by the upper portion of the iceberg, while the majority of the costs is invisible and is hidden under the water surface.

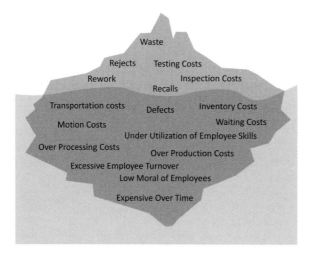

Figure 5 - *Costs iceberg (Krishnan, 2006)*

Costs of Poor Quality can be divided into the following categories:

Conformance Costs:
- Prevention Costs:
  Costs related to quality planning. This includes systems and procedures to prevent things going wrong like design reviews, in-process controls, employee training etc. Whilst beneficial, they are still actually costs related to quality and as such classified under CoPQ.

- Appraisal Costs:
  Costs related to quality control. This includes systems and procedures that exist only to check for problems like inspections and special systems or procedures to verify the quality.

Non-Conformance Costs:
- External Failure Costs:
  Costs related to defects that have reached the customer. They include all costs related to handling the customer complaint like repair or replacement of the bad good or service delivered to the customer.

- Internal Failure Costs:
  Costs related to quality problems within the organization, like yield loss (scrap), rework and the use of excessive resources.

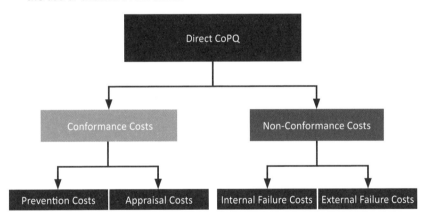

Figure 6 - *Direct Costs of Poor Quality*

1.5.2 Project selection
Low Hanging Fruit

A commonly used metaphor for doing the simplest or easiest work first is called 'Low-hanging fruit'. The low-hanging fruit presents the most obvious opportunities because they are readily achievable and do not require a lot of effort. In process improvement initiatives this may refer to problems with known solutions and low required investment, so problems that can be solved with very little effort. The issues that should have been solved a long time ago are represented by 'apples, rotting on the ground'.

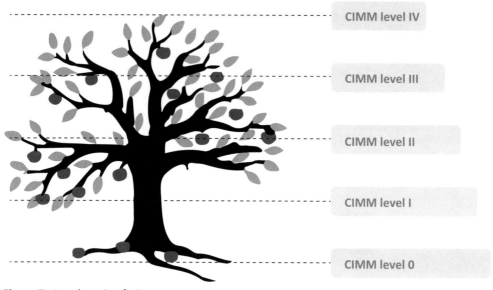

Figure 7 - *Low-hanging fruit*

Project Priority Diagram

Although Yellow Belts and Orange Belts are normally not involved in the selection process, it may be interesting to know the Project Priority Diagram. This is a simple but powerful technique that helps to prioritize projects. The diagram uses one dimension for 'Impact for the organization' (benefit) and a second dimension for 'Effort to achieve results'. It will make sense to start with projects that have a significant impact and can be realized with little effort.

1

1. Quick Wins – (High Impact, Low Effort): these are opportunities to choose first, as they give good return and require relatively little effort. These projects are called 'Low-hanging fruit' projects.

2. Major Projects – (High Impact, High Effort): these opportunities give good returns, but require a lot of effort. They take a long time to complete and can be complex to execute.

3. Not now – (Low Impact, Low Effort): do not worry too much about these opportunities, until resources become available. There are better opportunities to work on.

4. Don't do – (Low Impact, High Effort): avoid these opportunities, because they give low returns and they waste time which would be better used on something else.

In addition, a third dimension can be added to indicate if the team (or department) has the competencies to find the solutions and if it is empowered to implement the required solution. If this is the case, you can make the circle green, while the circle should be made red if this is not the case.

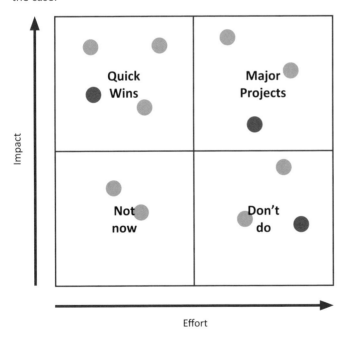

Figure 8 - *Project priority diagram*

"If you pick the right people and give them

the opportunity to spread their wings

and put compensation as a carrier behind it

you almost do not have to manage them."

- Jack Welch -

2

Process Improvement Deployment

2

Process Improvement Deployment reviews how process improvement programs should be deployed across the organization. Process Improvement Deployment is a process of continuous effort in keeping the organizational culture in line with the organizational goals.

For Green Belts, Black Belts and Management it is important to understand associated aspects of leadership, management of change and team development. These aspects show dynamics that can occur during a project such as cooperation, resistance, escalation of problems and solving roadblocks. For Yellow Belts and Orange Belts it is important to understand the dynamics that can occur during Lean Six Sigma programs and to understand that an organizations culture can influence the success of Lean Six Sigma deployment. This chapter will therefore review an introduction to management of change that is often an important element in process improvement programs.

2.1 Management of Change

Management of change is a much discussed, yet controversial term. Most people do not like change. However, we simply cannot do without change. Our lifestyle, our economy, even our culture is based on change. Without change we would still be chasing bears and living in caves. Within our organizations we simply have to deal with changes.

There is an everlasting flow of changing requests from customers, price pressure, technological innovations and competition. As a consumer we all want our TVs to get larger, thinner and cheaper. We all want our computers to become smaller, faster and (again) cheaper. A request for a passport and financial transactions need to go faster, and we all want more cures and care without paying more… At the same time, many people have problems when these changes have an impact on their way of working.

*"If you always do what you always did
you will always get what you always got."*

2.1.1 Organizational culture

Organizational culture is the behavior of humans within an organization as well as the meaning that people attach to this behavior. Organizational culture also represents the collective values, beliefs and principles of people, which is a product of aspects such as history, product, market, technology, strategy, type of employees, management style, and national culture (Needle, 2004). Organizational culture also includes the integrated pattern of shared knowledge and information and the capacity for learning and transferring knowledge to others. All these aspects comprise the organizational culture that affects the collective way of thinking and working by people in the organization and determine the standards and values of an organization. It affects the way people and groups interact with each other, with clients and with stakeholders.

A major reason why a process of change is difficult is because the organizational culture, and the structures in which it is embedded, often reflect the imprint of earlier periods in a persistent way. This may cause a remarkable level of inertia. Although the management of an organization acknowledges the importance of organizational culture in a process of change, there is clear diversity in the way they treat organizational culture. Management should be open to the signals sent by those who are part of the process of change. Taking into account the cultural aspects of the organization, it will be helpful in the acceptance of new improvement initiatives.

Figure 9 - *Management of change within the organization*

2.1.2 Change Management approaches

Major changes should always be started and continued Top-down. Also Green and Black Belt projects will follow a Top-Down approach. Even the first 5S implementation will be Top-down. However, programs of change cannot sustain for a longer period of time if improvement initiatives are only ever led Top-Down.

The expression 'Top-Down' means that all directions are provided from top management and that execution is done by senior staff. In this traditional management-style, objectives are established by management as well as guidelines, information, timing and budgets. The Bottom-up approach however, implies that the team is formed by work-floor staff. Managers are expected to communicate objectives and values rather than activities and detailed planning. A proactive input and execution as well as decisions about the course of action are taken by the team rather than by management. The team is encouraged and empowered to develop the steps necessary and to make their own choices of techniques and ways to achieve the expected results.

The Bottom-up approach will improve the agility and productivity of problem solving, especially for so-called 'Low-hanging fruit' projects where there is no need for management involvement to identify and implement solutions. Another advantage of the Bottom-up approach is that problems are solved by employees who are experiencing the problems every day. It is also in their benefit that these problems are solved, because it makes their lives easier. Very often it appears that employees think creatively and already have ideas on how to solve problems, but in traditional organizations the issue is that they are not encouraged and empowered to do so. Another advantage of the Bottom-up approach is that it involves the entire organization rather than having projects done by a small group of senior staff.

Empowering the work-floor in Level-I and Level-II projects, frees up time for senior staff to work on Level-III to Level-V breakthrough improvement projects. Although both approaches are needed, it appears that traditional organizations lack the Bottom-up approach, which is a roadblock for creating a powerful Continuous Improvement organization. It might take a while to break with the traditional management style and to introduce Bottom-up in the organization. But in the end it will be worth the time and effort as collaboration will become much more efficient, and team members will work together more productively. The Bottom-up approach will increase the motivation of employees as they are empowered, involved, responsible and appreciated.

A simple and straightforward approach, especially for bottom-up initiatives, is the '3D-process':

- Discuss: involving all concerned.
- Decide: by consensus.
- Do: following the group decision without repining.

This process requires that there is time given to all involved so that they can contribute to define the solution or new situation. After a certain period of time it is necessary to come to a decision. The best way to reach an agreement is by 'Consensus'. This means that the minority of the group will conform to the opinion of the majority of the group, without starting a new discussion. The entire team now contributes to the implementation of the agreed actions without repine.

"You do not have to see the whole staircase.

Just take the first step."

- *Martin Luther King jr.* -

3
Project Management

Most process improvement initiatives, at each of the maturity levels, are executed as a project by a team of people. Therefore it is important to discuss how to manage projects.

In this chapter we will review the way improvement projects should be managed. This starts with the identification of the team and the roles and responsibilities within the team. We will also cover a number of project management roadmaps, the identification of customers and their requirements, the Project Charter and a number of project management techniques.

Yellow and Orange Belts need to know the various roles and responsibilities, the different process improvement roadmaps and some project management techniques like the project charter and 'Voice of Customer'.

3.1 Team formation

Most process improvement projects, both small and large, are executed by teams and not by individuals. Therefore this section will review the different roles and responsibilities of individuals and stakeholders in these projects.

3.1.1 Roles and Responsibilities

There are several roles and responsibilities for all those involved in process improvement activities and programs. In this section, the various process improvement roles and responsibilities are explained. Depending on the size of the organization, one or more (Master) Black Belts are responsible for demonstrating and teaching the principles of Lean Six Sigma within the entire organization. They are supported by Green Belts, who execute improvement projects within the organization. The Orange and Yellow Belts support the projects as team members.

Champion
The Champion is the problem owner or the person who has identified the project. The Champion is involved in project selection and in assigning the project manager. The Champion is also the initiator of the Project Charter. There can be several Champions in an organization.
The Champion plays an important role in process improvement programs and is the sponsor of Lean Six Sigma projects. He is responsible for monitoring the project progress. The role of the Champion during the different project phases and Tollgate reviews is essential. He ensures that the project gets the proper priority and makes sure that any barriers for executing will be removed.

Master Black Belt
The Master Black Belt is a process improvement expert. He is responsible for deploying the overall Lean Six Sigma program and performs the internal training programs. The Master Black Belt will have at least 5 years of experience in executing projects himself. He will support management in selecting the breakthrough projects and the Green Belts and Black Belts in executing their projects. Within Lean Management the master of knowledge and expertise is called the Sensei.

Black Belt
Lean Six Sigma Black Belts are experts in executing Lean Six Sigma projects. As a program manager they are responsible for managing complex breakthrough projects and supporting improvement teams with tools and techniques. Very often Black Belts are full time assigned to process improvement programs. Black Belts have both skills for applying analytical tools and skills for leading change. The scope of the project can be across departments and organizations.

Green Belt
Lean Six Sigma Green Belts are specialists in executing Lean Six Sigma projects. With the right combination of specialist expertise, statistical analysis and structured Lean Six Sigma methodology, the Green Belt is able to achieve significant improvements in performance and quality. The impact on the organization and savings can be as large as a Black Belt project, but in general Green Belt projects have a smaller scope and are less complex than Black Belt projects. The scope of the project is often within one department, process or expertise rather than across departments. Green Belts might work alone or as a junior project manager in a team. Team members can be other Belts or employees without Lean Six Sigma competencies. Green Belts can also be team members in larger Black Belt projects.

Orange Belt
Lean Six Sigma Orange Belts are familiar with the Lean Six Sigma methodology and are able to apply problem solving and Lean tools. They have basic knowledge of statistical tools but will probably need the support of Green and Black Belts to apply these tools. Orange Belts are executing Kaizen and Lean projects or less complicated Six Sigma projects in their immediate environment. Orange Belts are often team leaders or supervisors with an in-depth knowledge of a process, product or equipment. Therefore they will also be valuable team members in Green or Black Belt projects.

Yellow Belt
When an organization decides to implement Lean Six Sigma company-wide, very often large groups of employees will be trained at the level of Yellow Belt to create a strong foundation. The Lean Six Sigma methodology and some of the tools are included. The type of tools depends on the improvement program. This is called 'Fit For Purpose' training. Yellow Belts are experienced with the processes in daily practice and are therefore the ideal leaders of Kaizen projects or valuable team members in Green or Black Belt projects. Activities can be collecting data, contribute to the development of standards or participate in brainstorm sessions.

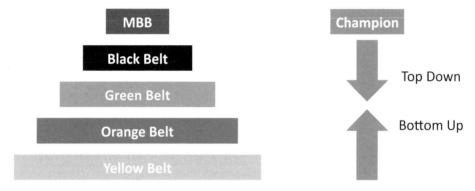

Figure 10 - *Lean Six Sigma Belt levels*

3.1.2 Team member selection

Working as a team means a group of individuals working collaboratively on achieving the same objective. Each of the team members is doing a part of the work while all of these sub-tasks contribute to the whole. Working with teams is a crucial part of an organization. Teamwork means that people will cooperate using their individual skills and provide constructive feedback, regardless of any conflicts between individuals. Working with multi-disciplinary teams brings together knowledge and skills from different individuals.

It is essential that team members are subject matter experts and that the collective sum of their expertise at least covers the whole of the process that is being improved. It is often helpful to also have on the team a subject matter expert who is a supplier and one who is a customer.

The selection of team members does not only depend on the type of a project, but also on the maturity level at which the organization is operating. Starting the first projects on the next maturity level requires different competencies in order to maintain a certain level. Since starting at a new maturity level is a project on its own, it requires a senior project manager. For instance, implementing 5S is not something to be managed by a junior employee or by an operator. Although the 5S tool itself is very simple, the process of implementing the 5S philosophy across a department or an organization requires Lean knowledge expertise and skills of project management and management of change.

The team formation and duration of projects depends very much on the type of project, the scope of the project and the state within a certain level. Implementing 5S across multiple departments in an environment that has no experience with 5S, can take half a year or even longer, while implementing 5S in one department within a company that has already got experience with 5S in other departments can be done in a few weeks. Implementing a new strategy, changing behavior of people, transforming processes or deploying new techniques will take much longer than sustaining a certain level or executing a single project. In general single projects on a higher level take more time than single projects on lower levels.

3.2 Process Improvement roadmaps

In this section we will review a number of commonly used project approaches and roadmaps. We will also review the differences and coherences between bottom-up projects and top-down projects. Taking into account the process improvement maturity model from the previous chapter, basically CIMM Level-I and CIMM Level-II projects tend to follow the PDCA roadmap and A3-report. The DMAIC approach is applied for CIMM Level-III and CIMM Level-IV projects, while the DMADV roadmap is followed at CIMM Level-V. Reviewing tis roadmap is out of scope of this book though. In addition some organizations (e.g. automotive) follow the 8D problem solving process for customer complaints.

3.2.1 Kaizen roadmap

Many small improvement projects, like Kaizen events and other Level-II initiatives, follow the PDCA approach. The PDCA abbreviation stands for Plan-Do-Check-Act and is also known as the Deming or Shewhart Cycle. We will briefly review each of the four steps:

Plan
Within the Plan-phase we will identify a relevant issue, followed by forming a team that has the knowledge and time to work on the problem and is empowered to implement the solution. We will define the problem description and establish the objectives. Then the problem will be analyzed and possible causes will be determined. Quality tools and brainstorm techniques like the Ishikawa (or Fishbone) diagram or 5-Whys can be used in this phase. Finally, the team will generate a solution and an implementation plan. The plan will be presented to the department leader to get approval to execute the plan.

Do
Within the Do-phase the team will execute the implementation plan and put in place the solutions that will take away the root cause. Data of the improved process will be collected.

Check
Within the Check-phase the team will compare the data of the improved process with the initial data. The team will measure the effect of the solution and verify if the root cause has indeed been eliminated. The team will also verify if the output of the improved process is what would be expected.

Act
Within the Act-phase the team will review whether the actions taken have achieved the right effect and if any additional actions need to be initiated. Second, the team has to sustain the established improvement. This is an important step to ensure that the process performance will not deteriorate over time again. This step is the wedge as shown in Figure 11. Without securing the improvement properly we will be certain to face the same problem again in the future.

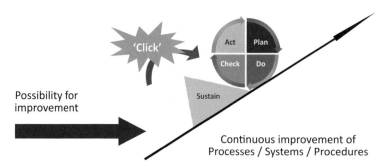

Figure 11 - *Continuous Improvement PDCA*

A3-report

One of the tools Toyota has been using to manage people to achieve operational learning and to present project results is the A3-report. The report is named after the international paper size (A3) on which it fits. It is a key tactic in sharing a deeper method of thinking that lies at the heart of Toyota's sustained success.

An A3 report is composed of a number of sequential boxes arrayed in a template. Often, the four steps of the PDCA process are followed and visualized in the A3-template. On the opposite page an A3 is presented of problems encountered within the translation process of documents. The project manager used the A3-approach to attack the problem while he was mentored by his supervisor.

1. Describe problem background.
2. Describe the current problem conditions.
3. Set the desired goals.
4. Analyze the situation to establish causality.
5. Define possible countermeasures.
6. Define the action plan to implement solution.
7. Define follow-up actions.

The objective of using A3s is twofold. The first is to solve the problem at hand. The ultimate goal however is to make the process of problem solving transparent and sharing the solution with others. It will create an organization full of thinking, learning problem solvers. The danger is that organizations do not use the tool in a proper way, but use it for window dressing. Keep in mind that the purpose is not to fill in the A3, but use it to communicate the solution to others in order to share knowledge.

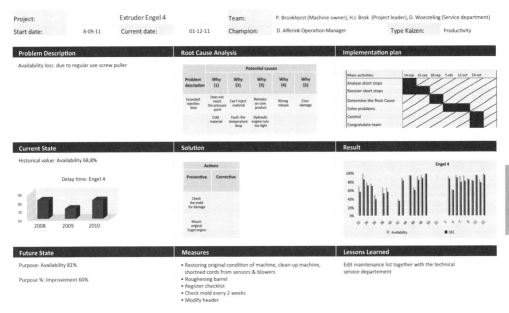

Figure 12 - *Example A3 report (John Shook, 2008)*

3.2.2 Problem Solving Process (8D)

The 'Eight Disciplines Problem Solving', also called '8D' or 'Global 8D', is a problem solving method. Its purpose is to identify, correct and eliminate problems. The 8D method is ideally suited to supply brief and concise reports to the customer in order to demonstrate how the problem was solved. The 8D methodology was originally created by the U.S. Department of Defense (1974). The methodology has been widely used by Ford in the automotive industry. Later on the methodology was applied in the entire automotive sector. If a series of components did not meet specifications, the customer would request an 8D from its supplier. Nowadays the 8D approach is applied more and more in other sectors as well.

Typically, an 8D request is triggered by a 'Non Conformity Report' (NCR), which is raised by the customer and received by the supplier of the problem. Because the steps in the process are defined, it is clear to the supplier what is expected. During the problem solving process, the customer and supplier can communicate about expectations and progress following these steps.

Table 3.1. *8D Problem solving process*

Step	Description
D0	Determine 'Emergency Response Action' (ERA)
D1	Establish the team
D2	Describe the problem
D3	Develop Interim Containment Action (ICA)
D4	Identify & Verify Root Cause
D5	Identify Permanent Corrective Action (PCA)
D6	Implement & Validate the PCA
D7	Prevent reoccurrence
D8	Congratulate the team

D0 – Emergency Response Action (ERA):
When a problem occurs, it is recommended to shut down the line immediately to prevent the production of huge piles of products that have the same failure. The 'Emergency Response Action' describes supplier actions on items already produced. These items may be found in several locations like the customer, plant or warehouse. ERA requires checking for errors in already manufactured items. Checked items should be marked in such a way that it is evident that these have been checked. The checked results should be documented. This activity is often 'quick and dirty'.

D1 – Establish the team:
When you receive a complaint from a customer, or a problem is experienced in the normal work environment, the first step is to establish a (multidisciplinary) team that has knowledge and is empowered to solve the problem.

D2 – Describe the problem:
The problem has to be described from the viewpoint of the problem holder as objectively and clearly as possible. It is important that no solutions are mentioned in the problem description. The problem should be sustained with data. Sometimes a separate form is used to report the deviation from the standard. This form is called a 'Non Conformity Report' (NCR).

D3 – Develop Interim Containment Actions(ICA):
The 'Interim Containment Action' (ICA) describes activities preventing material, produced after detection of the problem, from reaching the customer (in contrast to ERA (D0) describing material produced before detection of the problem). Especially for high volume production this is an important step. Shutting down the line however would mean that the customer, or the next line in the process, would not receive any parts. To prevent a total shut down, an Interim Containment Action needs to be defined to guarantee that good products are still going to be delivered, while at the same time no bad products will be delivered.

D4 – Identify & Verify Root Cause:
In this step we will determine the Root Cause. Sometimes simple problem solving techniques can be used such as the Fishbone diagram, Cause & Effect matrix or the 5-Whys technique. In the case of persistent and complicated problems, a full Six Sigma DMAIC project can be started to identify and eliminate the Root Causes.

D5 – Identify 'Permanent Corrective Action' (PCA):
The cause of the problem is now known. The next step is to establish corrective measures: the root cause must be eradicated. Permanent Corrective Action is the solution you finally want to implement in order to avoid the problem happening again. This is contrary to ERA and ICA where the solution is often limited to inspection and sorting of produced parts.

D6 – Implement & Validate the PCA:
The team now knows the solution to the problem. In this step the solution will be implemented and validated. Validation can be achieved by removing the solution and verifying if the problem expresses itself again. If you can switch the problem on and off, you know that you really have found the root cause as well as the solution.

D7 – Prevent reoccurrence:
To avoid the problem occurring again in the future, additional measures are usually necessary. In this step, the team should define a plan to ensure that the same problem will not reoccur in the future. This may result in changed specifications, operator training and updating quality documentation like PFMEA, Control plan and work instructions.

D8 – Congratulate the team:
The last step in the 8D methodology is to congratulate and reward the team. Delivering a good performance is worth a pat on the back.

3.2.3 DMAIC roadmap

DMAIC is an abbreviation for Define, Measure, Analyze, Improve and Control. DMAIC refers to a data-driven improvement initiative used for improving, optimizing and stabilizing business processes and products. The DMAIC roadmap offers a focused and structured approach to improve processes and solve problems in an organization. The roadmap is used mainly for Six Sigma projects (Level-IV). Lean projects (Level-III) use both PDCA as the DMAIC roadmap. Kaizen projects (Level-II) are advised to follow the PDCA roadmap because it is less complicated.

In the Define phase of the roadmap the operational problem is defined and the Project Charter (see section 3.4) as well as the 'Critical To Quality' metric (CTQ). In the Measure phase the measurement system that needs to measure the CTQ is validated. In the Analyze phase, the current process is analyzed and potential factors of influence are identified. In the Improve phase improvements are defined, implemented and verified. Finally in the Control phase measures will be put in place to sustain the improvements. Each of these phases will be discussed in more detail in the following sections.

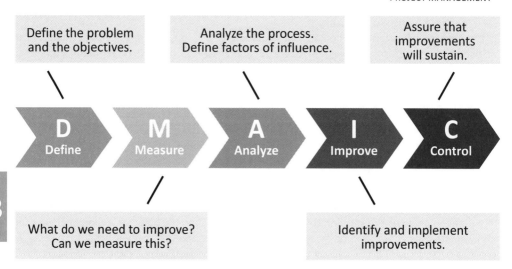

Figure 13 - *Lean Six Sigma DMAIC roadmap*

Project selection is formally not part of the DMAIC roadmap, but should be done prior to the start-up of a Lean Six Sigma project. The Champion or management selects a project based on selection criteria such as size, impact and urgency. However, it might be that during the evaluation in the first phases the project scope or team will be changed. Sometimes a quick DMA is done prior to the actual start of a full DMAIC project. Portfolio management and project prioritization are also not part of the DMAIC roadmap itself, but are managed at a higher level by the Champion or by the Master Black Belt.

Define:
Every Lean Six Sigma project starts with the Define phase. General Electric added the Define phase to the original MAIC methodology. Based on the problem statement and the scope of the project, a team is formed and a project manager is assigned. The Champion is the project owner.

The purpose of the Define phase is to clearly define the problem statement, the goals, the scope and the high-level project timeline. These elements will be combined in a Project Charter [see paragraph 3.4].

The problem should be linked to the external customer (Voice of Customer), the organization (Voice of Business) and to other stakeholders (Voice of Stakeholder). At the start of the project a Project Charter will be written that incorporates all these items [see section 3.4]. The Define phase helps to clarify the understanding of why the problem is actually a problem. This is expressed as a financial measure. This is important before resources and effort are invested in the project.

The problem definition is done from the perspective of external client (Voice of Customer) and / or from the perspective of the organization (Voice of Business). In the Define phase it is determined which metric can be linked to the problem of the customer. These so-called "Critical to Quality (CTQ) is the common thread throughout the DMAIC project. Each Six Sigma project focuses on a limited number of CTQs. To determine the CTQs, a CTQ Flowdown is composed [see paragraph 7.1]. Within Lean projects the CTQ is often related to quantities or time (lead time, delivery time, processing time, capacity utilization, etc.).

Measure:
Within the Measure phase the gap between the current performance and the required performance is defined. The purpose of the Measure phase is to make customer requirements tangible and measurable. Determining the measurement procedure and validating the measurement equipment are the main purposes of the Measure phase. This is the heart of any DMAIC improvement project. It is decided what should be measured and how it is measured.

In the Measure phase is determined that the measurement procedure is and how well the measurement system is able to measure the CTQs. It is important that the team ensures that the measurement system, and the data collected are valid and reliable before proceeding with the Analyze phase of the project. In order to give a ruling on this, a 'Measurement System Analysis' (MSA) is conducted, mostly by Green or Black Belts, on the measurement system [see paragraph 7.5]. Often people rate the Measure phase as the most difficult stage in a DMAIC project, because data is sometimes not available, and carrying out a MSA is difficult. Within Lean projects it is very important to clearly define the definitions of the CTQ and the source for the data, so there is no debate about the performance.

Analyze:
The goal of any Six Sigma project is to get the CTQ on target and to reduce the variation of the CTQ. The purpose of the Analyze phase is to identify, validate and to identify factors that have influence on the variation. These factors need to be adjusted or eliminated.

In the Analyze phase, the relationships are established between the CTQ (also called 'Key Process Output variables', Responses or 'Ys') and the 'Key Process Inputs variables' (also called 'Xs'). Often, a large number of potential influence factors are identified at the beginning of this phase, for example by a brainstorm session. The number of potential factors of influence is then reduced by carrying out screening experiments. Next, a hypothesis is determined, and experiments are being performed in order to test the hypothesis. The result is a (mathematical) model that represents the relationships between the factors of influence (X1..n) and the CTQ. Within Lean projects in this phase, a 'Value Stream Map – Current State' or 'Spaghetti diagram' of the current state is drawn to highlight Waste and opportunities for improvement.

Improve:
The purpose of the Improve phase is to implement and verify solutions to the problem. To determine the optimum settings for a process, several tools can be utilized (e.g. Regression analysis or Design of Experiments). A verification study is advised before changes will be made to the process. Within Six Sigma projects often a Process Capability Analysis [see section 7.8] is performed to investigate the performance of the improved process.

Within Lean a 'Value Stream Map – Future State' will be composed. This is a design of a new process flow or factory layout. TPM or 5S initiatives and Kaizen projects can be performed to eliminate Waste or to resolve quality issues.

Control:
The purpose of the Control phase is to sustain the achieved results. Although the problem has been fixed by now, the team should not forget to take this phase seriously to prevent the problem to occur again. The best way to accomplish this is to capture the improvement by applying 'Poka Yoke' [see section 6.8.3], to guarantee that the process is independent of the way of working. Improvements should be monitored to ensure sustainable success. To achieve this, a Control plan should be composed, work instructions should be updated and employees should be trained.

The team should verify if the forecasted savings have been met and should report the 'Lessons Learned', so the next project can benefit from this experience. Then the assignment is formally returned to the Champion. Finally, the task of the Champion or department manager is to appreciate the team for their achievements.

In addition to the DMAIC roadmap some organizations also apply an additional step, called Replication. The purpose of the Replicate phase is to determine other products or processes that might gain advantage from the achievements. Replicating the improvements, sharing lessons learned and team appreciation helps to build buy-in for future DMAIC or improvement initiatives.

DMAIC 14 step roadmap
The five DMAIC phases are followed by all Lean Six Sigma Belts across the world. Because all of the steps are very comprehensive these phases are split into a number of steps. There are many different variants of these roadmaps. In Table 3.2. an example is given of a 14 step DMAIC roadmap (Source: Minitab Quality Companion).

Table 3.2. *DMAIC roadmap*

Define	1	Define and Scope project
	2	Define defect
	3	Plan and document project
Measure	4	Evaluate measurement system
	5	Establish baseline
	6	Set improvement goals
Analyze	7	Map process and identify inputs
	8	Isolate key inputs
	9	Develop $Y=f(X)$ function
Improve	10	Determine optimum settings
	11	Implement proposed improvement
	12	Validate proposed improvement
Control	13	Implement control strategy
	14	Close out project

3.3 Voice of Customer

Many projects start with a customer complaint or quality problem. It can also be an internal problem, like a high fall-out rate at a machine or a logistical bottleneck in the process. Hence we need to understand why the problem is actually a problem to the customer. Even if you think a good product was delivered, it might not meet the customer's expectation or specification. You can try to convince the customer that the product meets the quality standards, but you can also try to understand the customer and be grateful for the opportunity he is giving you to improve your process. Each improvement project must ensure it is customer focused.

3.3.1 Customer identification

Any Lean Six Sigma project is taking the Voice of the Customer as a starting point. Even in smaller projects the customer should always be the starting point. Defining what will be the benefit for the customer is a critical initial step of every improvement project as it nails down the commitment of what should be delivered at the end of the project.

Both external clients, customers, competitors, shareholders and other stakeholders expect us to become better, cheaper and faster continuously. They all drive the Continuous Improvement efforts we work on. In general we distinguish two groups of customers. The first group are the external clients and customers to whom we deliver our products and services. They desire products and services according specifications, at competitive pricings and at agreed timings. This determination is called the 'Voice of the Customer' (VOC). The drive from the second group is the internal drive from shareholders, executive management, employees or internal departments. Their desire is mostly about a safe work environment, internal delivery times, no mistakes, good work environment, employee satisfaction, new business opportunities and cost reductions. Furthermore we have to take into account regulatory requirements, durability and environment. The determination of the needs for this second group is called the 'Voice of the Business' (VOB). Some drivers may be important for both groups while other drivers may be important for one of the two groups. In all cases improvement projects have to consider the 'Voice' of both groups. In case they are contradictory, the Voice of the Customer is generally given a higher priority than the Voice of the Business.

3.3.2 Customer requirements

To understand your customer requirements, you need to become a customer. Call your own call center, buy your own product and be critical to yourself. Go out to meet your customer or perform a survey. Do not be afraid of the outcome, because it might lead to improvement opportunities. You can also do this internally in your own organization. In the TV series 'Undercover Boss', a director of a huge company goes undercover to the work-floor, talking to employees to really understand what is going on.

In order to understand what is necessary to satisfy our customer we can ask the following questions:

- Who is the customer?
- What do we provide to our customer?
- What is important to our customers' needs, wishes and demands?
- Is the process focused on the needs of the customer?

3.4 Project Charter

At the start of larger projects, generally at level III to V, a Project Charter will be produced. This is a document agreed between the Champion and the project manager which include the problem description, scope, objectives, timing, budget and resources. The Project Charter should clarify the business case and the need of the specific project. It should mention the product or service and the customer concerned.

3.4.1 Problem statement

The problem description should never mention a solution to the problem, because if a solution is known a problem solving project is not needed. Lean Six Sigma projects are focusing on solving problems not on implementing known solutions like buying a new piece of equipment. Ensure that the problem statement is SMART:

- Specific: Precise statement of the problem and goal.
- Measurable: Ability to measure the performance (both problem and solution).
- Attainable: Objectives are reasonable and goals can be achieved.
- Relevant: The problem is urgent or has an impact on the organization.
- Timely: Solutions can be achieved in reasonable time.

If the problem description is not SMART, the project is likely to go down the path of fixing the wrong things causing additional pain to the organization. Example: "Ever since John came to work here the organization has been going down-hill" or "We can solve the quality issues by buying a new machine." These are examples of ignorant problem definitions, not likely to build consensus or to chart a course for solving real problems. Although regularly the Champion, Black Belt and Green Belt are responsible to compose the Project Charter, even the Yellow and Orange Belts should understand the importance of defining the problem specifically and quantitatively, before blindly going down a path of fixing the wrong problem, or not fixing anything at all. Using structured methods like DMAIC and simple guidelines like SMART will help you achieve success and avoid disappointing results.

3.4.2 Project Scope and Goal

For both large improvement projects as for small Kaizen events, it is important to agree on the scope of the project in an early phase. It is relevant to agree on expectations of all involved to assure that the project will be completed within time and budget. The scope of a project means the development of a common understanding as to what is included in the project and what is excluded. Therefore it is not only relevant to define what is in scope, but also what is out of scope.

A change in scope may cause problems, especially when the champion and the project leader had different perception of what was in scope. For instance, the project leader might believe that the team should focus on a specific area (e.g. product, machine, department, client, etc.), while the champion thought that the team was working on a different area.

The scope of a project may be changed during the progress of the project, but only if all stakeholders are involved in the change and the redefinition of the new scope. All should realize that a change in scope will have an impact on time and budget of the project.

Project Charter

Business unit:	**Project Leader:**	**Belt level / Method:**
Department	Name of project leader	GB/BB & DMAIC/DMADV

Project title:	**Project Number:**
Short name of the project	Project number assigned

Problem Statement:

Short description of the problem / Reason for the project

Product / Service:	**Process:**	**Customer:**
What is delivered?	Operational process	Who receives the product?

Hard Benefits:

Direct bottom-line savings   ☐ Benefit Enabler   ☐ Benefit Realisation

Hard Benefits /yr:	**Budget:**	**Net Savings /yr:**
Direct Monetary savings	Estimated investment costs	Savings minus Costs

Soft Benefits:

Risk avoidance and Nonmonetary benefits

Interface with other projects:

Is the project part of another project? Will the project impact another device or customer?

Start Date:	**Target Completion Date:**	**Actual Closure Date:**
Date the team will start	Completion of Control / Verify	Release of team

Figure 14 - *Example Project Charter (LSSA, 2009)*

3.4.3 Project performance measures

There can be several elements that drive improvement projects. Each of these elements should address at least one of the following focus points:

- Quality   products/services according to specifications.
- Delivery   products/services at agreed timings.
- Cost   products/services at competitive pricings.

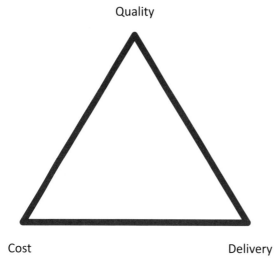

Figure 15 - *Project focus points*

Quality can be improved by increasing effectiveness and capability of the process, Costs can be reduced by increasing efficiency and productivity. In the end, a higher quality performance and delivery performance will also lead to lower costs.

3.4.4 Project benefits calculation

It is common that a project will be initiated due to some overt failures to meet one of the project performance measures. This leads us to understand where the benefits are likely to be realized. For example, if our customers are switching to a competitor because our delivery time is too long, then a project to reduce delivery time might be launched. The gap between current delivery performance and the target delivery performance is then used to project the target benefits. These benefits can be classified in the following three categories:

1 - Hard Benefits (direct & indirect):
Eliminating Waste and reducing the amount of Non-Value Adding activities can be quantified in terms of hard benefits to the organization in the form of reduces labor costs, resource savings and reduces Work in Process. These are called direct hard benefits.
As a consequence of a more efficient process and less WIP it is likely that fewer mistakes will be made. A shorter lead time will produce a more responsive service which will lead to improved reputation. These are called indirect hard benefits.

2- Soft Benefits:
Happier employees and an improved brand reputation are both examples of soft benefits. Soft benefits can be measured best through employee and survey responses. It is difficult to assign a monetary value to soft benefits, so they may not appear in the benefit calculation.

3 - Risk or Loss Avoidance Benefits:
Improving the lead time and preventing bad quality may prevent the loss of customers to the competitor. In this case a loss avoidance benefit may be included in the calculation so long as the records or measures to support the assertion is plausible. These benefits are likely to take the form of an estimate of the number of customers that would have been lost if the improvements had NOT taken place, multiplied by the average profit earned from a customer.

3.5 Project Management Techniques

This section sets out a number of tools and techniques that have to be taken into account during project execution. Yellow and Orange Belts are expected to attend meetings and come prepared. Yellow and Orange Belts often attend risk assessment meetings because the contribution of the work floor is important for process improvement and identification of risks.

3.5.1 Time management

Time management is the process of planning and execution of activities needed to complete certain deliverables within a certain time frame. Proper time management is an important element of personal efficiency. Those who are not able to manage their time effectively will not be able to meet expectations or have a great risk of facing a nervous breakdown. Time management include the following elements:

- Defining deliverables that need to be derived.
- Setting of priorities.
- Defining due dates for deliverables.
- Defining the quality level of deliveries.
- The process of balancing activities and available resources.
- Carrying out activities to compose deliverables.
- The process of monitoring progress.
- Team meetings to review status and dividing actions.
- The process of increasing efficiency of execution.
- Incentives to modify behavior to ensure deliveries within time.

A person is most productive when his mind is clear, free of things people commit to do which remain undone and become a drag on the unconscious mind (David Allen, 2001). The advice therefore is to clear your mind, by writing actions on your 'To do' list.

The most disturbing factor in the office is the email inbox. New emails coming in every few minutes bringing new information or that require new action. If you are not careful, your inbox will fully will dictate your daily schedule and your head is trying to keep up with all this information. It is therefore recommended to define fixed slots during the day for checking new emails.

If an action takes less than 2 minutes, do it right away. If the action will take longer than 2 minutes, consider it a project and add it to your 'To do' list. If possible, prioritize the items on your 'To do' list and add the amount of time needed to complete the action. Adding actions to your 'To do' list will free up your mind, making you more productive.

Several books have been published on Time management. One of these books is 'Getting Things Done' form David Allen (2001). 'Getting Things Done' is part tools and techniques, part psychology. This approach helped many to improve their personal productivity in today's hectic time.

3.5.2 Project progress

Project planning or project scheduling is an important element of project management. The objective is to achieve the predefined project goals within time, budget and quality. This includes the completion of project deliverables within a certain time frame (start date and completion date) by means of resources and activities.

An effective way of documenting an improvement project is through the use of a storyboard. Storyboards originated in the motion picture industry to help directors and cinematographers get a film's scene in sequence in a more visual way. Such storyboards resemble cartoon strips. A storyboard is a presentation on the wall or on a one page A1 poster. It is a chronological graphical presentation from the problem description to the solution. Lean Six Sigma project storyboards should follow the PDCA or DMAIC roadmap.

The storyboard is updated as the project progresses and is used to explain the project to colleagues and management. As such, it can also be used to promote and explain the Lean Six Sigma approach in general. The advantage is that project review meetings are done as stand-up-meetings at the shop floor (Gemba). This will save time and give the opportunity to involve employees and have a look at the process, product or equipment.

Team members of the project are advised to prepare a so-called 'Elevator pitch'. This reflects the idea that it should be possible to narrate a summary of the project in the time span of an elevator ride (approximately thirty seconds to two minutes).

Figure 16 - *Example Project Storyboard*

DMAIC Tollgate meeting

The DMAIC methodology for Lean Six Sigma projects is accomplished in five phases (Define, Measure, Analyze, Improve and Control). Regularly a Tollgate review session is scheduled between each phase by the project manager (Green Belt or Black Belt) to present the progress to the Champion or Project board. During this meeting all results within a certain phase are presented.

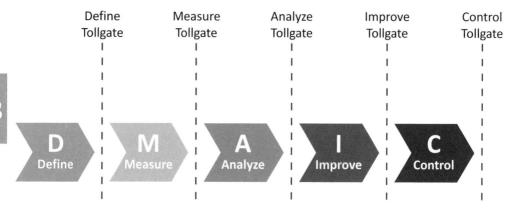

Figure 17 - *Lean Six Sigma DMAIC with Tollgate reviews*

3.5.3 Project Risk Management

Project Risk management is an important aspect within project management. A project risk is defined as an unintended event or condition with a certain probability and a certain negative effect on the project's objectives. Project objectives are often related to time, costs, quality or technology. Project Risk management is the identification, assessment and mitigation of risks. Risks can be identified in a brainstorm session by the team. The assessment can be done to qualify the probability and severity of each risk.

A pro-active approach to project planning, monitoring of risks and the identification and development of mitigating actions is the key to assuring the objectives of the project. Therefore it is good practice to maintain regular project plan reviews.

3

"Quality is everyone's responsibility."

- W. Edwards Deming -

4

CIMM Process Level I
Creating a solid foundation

Before organizations can really work on process improvement programs like Lean and Six Sigma, it is required that a proper foundation is put in place. The first level of any Continuous Improvement scenario starts with the objectives of a professional and safe work environment, Standardized Work and a solid quality management system. These elements will guarantee a stable foundation for further improvement initiatives.

In this chapter we will review how to build a solid foundation that is important for all other improvement strategies. We will review 5S to create an organized, professional and safe work environment. We will also discuss the importance of Standardized Work. Finally we will review the need for Quality Control & Quality Assurance. The role of Yellow and Orange Belts is very important in these kind of projects. They often lead these type of process improvement initiatives.

4.1 Organized Work Environment

The workspace is the mirror of the organization. If the surroundings are not organized, it reflects poorly on the organization and represents the way it regards its customers and their products or services. A tidy workspace leads to quality and is therefore the starting point for every improvement!

4.1.1 Organized Work Environment (5S)

5S is about smart workspace organization ('Good Housekeeping'). Employees are made familiar with the methodology and companies are assisted in the actual realization of a more structured working environment. As mentioned earlier: the workspace is the mirror of the organization and is the starting point for every improvement initiative. All employees directly or indirectly involved in the improvement project on the work floor should be involved in this process. The 5S technique itself is not very complicated, but because all employees will be involved and it requires a change in behavior, it will take quite some effort to implement 5S properly.

The 5S technique exposes waste and prevents it from reoccurring in the future. It supports the communication process of operational standards of the organization to all employees. It will result in an improved workplace efficiency, a professional representation to clients and a safer and more pleasant work environment. The process of implementing good housekeeping consists of 5 consecutive steps:

Table 4.1. *5S steps*

Japanese	English	Description
S1: Seiri	Sort	Only necessary items are at the workplace
S2: Seiton	Straighten	Everything has a fixed place
S3: Seiso	Shine	Everything is constantly kept clean
S4: Seiketsu	Standardize	Procedures and standards are visible
S5: Shitsuke	Sustain	Procedures are followed with discipline

Figure 18 - *Organized work environment 5S*

S1: Sort (Seiri)

The goal of the sorting step is to distinguish between what is necessary and what is superfluous. What is necessary, what can we get rid of? In this first step you make sure that only items that you regularly need are present at the work location. Items that are superfluous get in the way of the real work and potentially make the workplace unsafe. These items should be thrown away or removed to other areas.

Figure 19 - *5S example office environment (before and after)*

The 'Red tag procedure' can be used to support this process. A Red tag will be attached to items that are identified to be superfluous and to items for which it is not clear what to do with them. Anyone can change the description on the tag. After a few days, when each person has had the chance to modify the remarks on the red tag, the decision can be made to throw away or to remove the item to a designated location. After this first cleaning action, the remaining items and tools should be cleaned. Also broken lighting, furniture and equipment should be repaired. In service environments this step will focus on emptying the desk by throwing away documents and by cleaning out archives and cabinets. Second we can focus on deleting unnecessary data on computers and servers.

Figure 20 - *5S Red tag cards*

The Sort step is an important step and it certainly will make a significant difference. However, some might think that after this first cleaning action 5S is completed and implemented, but it is just the beginning.

S2: Straighten (Seiton)

After the cleaning out process in the first step, we will continue with the second step called 'Straighten'. The objective of this step is to identify a permanent location for each item. The work location should be organized in a way that everyone can find everything needed quickly and easily. Items that belong together, such as pencils, documents and tooling, should be combined and grouped. Items should be placed in the correct order (e.g. next to each other) to improve the flow of the process and to reduce errors.

> *"A place for everything and everything in its place."*
> *Benjamin Franklin*

It should be clear for everyone where to find an item and where to put it back in place after use. Especially important is that everything has a defined place and the most frequently used items are at hand. Locations of items should be visualized by means of outlining /marking. Visual methods can be used such as lines, markers, signs, arrows, color codes etc. Labels are often used to explain the system at a glance. A shadow board is often used in manufacturing and operation rooms. This makes it visually obvious when items are missing.

Figure 21 - *5S example organized workplace*

Also in this step we will arrange items based on the frequency of use. Items that are needed several times a day should be closer to the work location than items that are only used once a week. Items that are used even less frequent should be stored in a closet, separate department or warehouse.

Table 4.2. *5S where to keep items*

Frequency	Where to keep	Maximum distance
Continuously	On the body	Max. 50 cm
Every hour	At the workplace	Max. 1 meter
Every day	Close to the workplace	Max. 5 meter
Every week	At the department	Max. 10 meter
Every month	Central warehouse	Max. 250 meter
Every year	Regional warehouse	-
Less than once a year	Do you need it?	-

S3: Shine (Seiso)

This Shine step means that everything is in its place. The objective of this step is not to <u>make</u> everything clean, but to <u>keep</u> everything clean and orderly. Keeping a computer clean is not a physical thing necessarily, but involves keeping the directories organized and free of unnecessary or 'dirty' files.

4

The cleaning of the workplace should become routine. This means that it should be defined what should be cleaned, in what way it should be cleaned, when it should be cleaned and by whom it should be cleaned. Cleaning is a task for everyone, not just for the cleaning department. Why is this important? In a clean environment problems or faults become visible faster. By keeping the workplace clean you see deviations and you can prevent errors and mistakes. A clean environment also results in a safer work environment. Cleaning actually also means 'make it shine'. A shiny floor or a fresh painted wall will improve the working atmosphere and a person's mood. You probably recognize that you are more careful if you wear white clothes. White is very prone to dirt and that's exactly the point. Any contamination should be cleaned immediately. Every source of contamination will become visible and should be removed. A workspace should look like an operating room. Everyone knows inside an operating room the people keep the workplace pristine.

"Take 5 minutes at the end
of each day/shift for cleaning."

In the Shine step the illumination of the working area, noise and ergonomics should be given attention too. Flickering lights or working in an environment with insufficient illumination or working in a very noisy environment can result in overlooking items, stress and fatigue. Broken chairs, bad computer screens and or bad ergonomics can cause health complaints or even sickness.

Figure 22 - *5S ergonomics & safety*

4

S4: Standardize (Seiketsu)
The Standardize step addresses the question: 'How do we ensure constancy?' Standardization and guidelines for 5S is of great importance. In this step we will determine the rules and standards. This involves standards for cleaning and defining responsibilities.

After the first round of cleaning in step one, it is good to consider what you would do in the future and what should be in the cleaning program. Keeping a workplace clean only takes a few minutes a day. For example introducing a routine to clean up every last 5 minutes of a working day or shift.

To improve safety, fire extinguishers, first aid kits and exits should be marked clearly. Also standards should be defined for operator clothing like wearing safety glasses, hand gloves, sound protection and protective footwear.

Figure 23 - *Example Standardized industry environment (before and after)*

4.2 Organised work environment (5S)_2 VS.png	6.2.3 Takt Time, Cycle Time & Lead Time_3.png	6.5 Reducing Muda (Waste)_8.p
5.1.2 Root Cause Analysis (RCA).png	6.2.4 Measurement methods.png	6.5 Reducing Muda (Waste)_9.p
5.2.1 Check Sheet.png	6.2.4 Overall Equipment Effectiveness (OEE)_1.png	6.6.1 Flow 01.png
5.2.8 Box plot_1.png	6.2.4 Overall Equipment Effectiveness (OEE)_2.png	6.6.1 Flow 02.png
5.2.8 Box plot_2.png	6.2.4. Availability Rate 2.png	6.6.1 Flow 03.png
5.3.1 Affinity Diagram.png	6.2.6 Qualitative data vs. Quantitative data_2.png	6.6.3 Work balancing_1.png
5.3.2 5-Why_s.png	6.2.7 Qualitative data versus Quantitative data .png	6.6.3 Work balancing_2.png
5.3.3 Ishikawa diagram.png	6.4 FIFO.png	6.6.4 Competence managemen
5.3.4 Cause & Effect Matrix.png	6.4 Push.png	6.6.5 Total Productive Maintena
6.1 Process Mapping.png	6.4 Supermarket.png	6.6.6 Theory of Constraints (TOⁿ
6.1.1 Process Flow Diagram.png	6.4 VSM Lead Time.png	6.7 Reducing Mura (Unevennes
6.1.2 Spaghetti Diagram.png	6.4 Withdrawel.png	6.7.1 Pull_1.png
6.1.3 Swimlane Flowchart_1.png	6.5 Reducing Muda (Waste).png	6.7.1 Pull_2.png
6.1.3 Swimlane Flowchart_2.png	6.5 Reducing Muda (Waste)_2.png	6.7.2 Kanban_1.png
6.1.4 SIPOC_1.png	6.5 Reducing Muda (Waste)_3.png	6.7.2 Kanban_2.png
6.1.4 SIPOC_2.png	6.5 Reducing Muda (Waste)_4.png	6.7.4 Scheduling the Pacemakeⁿ
6.2.1 Effectiveness versus Efficiency.png	6.5 Reducing Muda (Waste)_5.png	6.7.5 Volume levelling.png
6.2.3 Takt Time, Cycle Time & Lead Time_1.png	6.5 Reducing Muda (Waste)_6.png	6.7.6 Type levelling_3.png
6.2.3 Takt Time, Cycle Time & Lead Time_2.png	6.5 Reducing Muda (Waste)_7.png	6.7.6 Type levelling_4.png

Figure 24 - *Example Standardized transactional environment (file naming structure)*

S5: Sustain (Shitsuke)
The final step is about sustaining all previous steps and actions. Without this step everything will revert to the original situation within a short space of time, untidy and potentially unsafe. Measures should be taken to guarantee that the new behaviors will be maintained.

Everyone is required to follow the agreed disciplines and procedures. Obviously management should lead by example. All employees have the obligation to indicate to others if the agreed procedures are not being followed.

Using an audit checklist ensures that objective monitoring can take place regularly and that results are measurable with a points score. Audit results and targets should be reported and published. The 5S score for a department is often represented by a spider diagram on the visual management board.

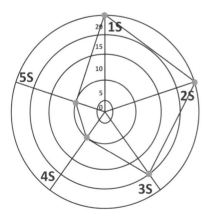

Figure 25 - *5S audit spider diagram*

4.2 Standardized Work

The Japanese method of process improvement is pretty straightforward. A Japanese auditor will ask you: 'Has a standard for this process been defined?' If the answer is no, the auditor will tell you that a standard needs to be defined. If the answer is yes, the next question will be: 'Are you working according the standard?' and 'What is your plan to improve the standard?'

1. If we have no standards, we need to develop them.
2. If we have standards, we should work according to the standards.
3. If we work according to the standards, we should continuously try to improve the standards.

4.2.1 Standardized Work and Documentation

Following this philosophy, it is important that standards defined in the quality management system are not just listed in a dusty book that is only brought out for audits. They should be visible and attainable for everybody in the organization. Standardized Work is applicable everywhere and necessary to create a solid foundation.

> *"Without a standard there is no logical*
> *basis for making a decision or taking action."*
> *Joseph Juran*

When using Standardized Work, we define who is trained and permitted to operate the process and how many people it takes to operate the process. Standardized Work also documents what is needed to start the process. For each operation step a 'Standard Operating Procedure' (SOP) is composed. The SOP is more than a work instruction document. The SOP is created by the employees together, by agreeing on the best way to operate the process. They should all agree, by applying consensus if needed, on the best way. Then this will become the standard and all will follow accordingly. Managers should generally defer to employees when determining the content of the SOP, as employees are usually more knowledgeable about the process than anyone else. They are also the ones who have to commit to the Standardized Work.

The SOP describes what items or tools are required and the sequence of the process activities. The SOP also clearly describes what the final product should look like and what quality checks need to be performed on the product. This will prevent the need for each employee to determine by himself what quality criteria the product or service should meet. The SOP procedure mentions the Cycle Time for the process step, which means that it is defined how long the employee is expected to work at the operation step before the product should be passed on to the next operation step.

Standardized Work also includes how much raw materials or components should be on hand at the operational step and how often component levels must be replenished. It also includes how often products are retrieved from the work cell and how they should be packed or stored. For service organizations Standardized Work includes how information should be documented and archived at the server. It also includes what standard documents, templates and revision numbers should be used.

The SOP documents the best practices to the current moment, but it can always be questioned and employees should always look for further improvement opportunities. Lean and Kaizen encourage the questioning of Standardized Work and looking for improvements. If one employee thinks he has found a better way, he should discuss this with his colleagues in order to update the current standard if his proposal should become the new standard.

Standardized Work does not have to be in conflict with flexibility or customization. On the contrary, a good example is the design of a new hospital. Each patient room was designed and shaped exactly the same, to use it for all types of treatment and care, to increase the flexibility of the room. The room was designed in collaboration with experts from different departments to assure all special requirements were incorporated in the final design.

Training Within Industry
A practical approach to establish and maintain standardized work is 'Training Within Industry' (TWI). This is a program of hands-on learning and practice, teaching essential skills for supervisors, team leaders, and anyone who directs the work of others. TWI has a long history of success in both industrial and transactional environments and is an essential element of Lean and Continuous Improvement programs. TWI generates cooperation and positive employee relations; it teaches supervisors how to quickly and correctly train employees and is used to solve problems efficiently and effectively. TWI consist of the flowing three pillars:

1 - Job Relation (JR):
Job Relations teaches the foundations of positive employee relations. Developing and maintaining these good relationships prevents problems from arising and is paramount to earn loyalty and cooperation from others.

2 - Job Instruction (JI):
Job Instruction is designed to develop basic stability of processes by implementing 'Standardized Work'. This program teaches the method to instruct employees how to perform a job correctly, safely and conscientiously. As is frequently the case, most processes are performed by various workers using different methods. Job Instruction requires how to identify the 'One best way' and to teach the process to this one way. The basis of stability is generated by doing the same thing the same way across all employees.

3 - Job Methods (JM):
Job Methods develops individuals to breakdown jobs into their constituent operations. Every detail is questioned in a systematic manner to generate ideas for improvement. The improved standard is developed by eliminating wasteful tasks, combining and rearranging necessary tasks and by simplifying required tasks.

One Point Lesson

SOP documents may be supplemented by One Point Lessons / Single Point Lessons. A 'One Point Lesson' (OPL) or 'Single Point Lesson' (SPL) is a structured teaching tool at the Gemba, explaining a single topic on one single (plasticized) sheet. OPLs originated from 'Total Productive Maintenance' (TPM) as a method to teach, instruct and warn operators. OPLs are an effective training tool. It is important that the OPL is written as simply as possible. Pictures, drawings and diagrams are preferred above texts. OPLs can support and simplify instructions and procedures but it is not the intention they replace Work instructions or SOPs.

OPLs are used:

- to warn about a dangerous situation;
- to explain the setup or maintenance of equipment;
- to describe the approach and measurement of an improvement initiative;
- to assure that everyone knows about a better way of doing something.

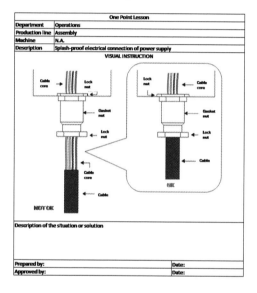

Figure 26 - *Example One Point Lesson*

4.3 Quality Management

Each organization needs to ensure that customer satisfaction is assured by meeting the demands and requirements of its clients. Organizations should also meet the legal requirements. Each organization should be able to manage its business processes properly. The quality procedures should be made known to all employees and they should work according to the agreed procedures.

4.3.1 Quality Management System

To give interpretation to quality management most companies implemented a 'Quality Management System' (QMS). A Quality Management System is a collection of all kind of business processes focused on achieving the quality policy and quality objectives to meet customer and legal requirements. There are different standards for quality management systems, but ISO 9001 is one of the most widely used systems in the world today. Over one million organizations worldwide are independently ISO 9001 certified.

Quality management can be divided into the following three groups of activities:

4

- Quality Planning (QP):
  Focused on planning how to fulfill the quality policy and translating that into measurable objectives and requirements. A sequence of steps are laid down for realizing them within a certain time frame.
- Quality Control (QC):
  Focused on detection of mistakes. Inspections and approvals that are applied in the realization process to ensure only good products and services will be delivered to the next process step or the final customer.
- Quality Assurance (QA):
  Focused on prevention. Not only preventing defects in delivered products and services, but also preventing all kind of problems in the company's processes by preparations and inline control measures.

Quality Planning

Quality Planning defines everything a company is going to do, to ensure the quality to the customer. Creating a Quality Management Plan is the first step in the quality management process. It is essential to provide the customer with confidence that his requirements will be met. Examples of Quality Planning are:

- Formulating the quality policy
- Identifying the customers' requirements.
- Listing the deliverables to be produced.
- Setting quality targets for these deliverables.
- Defining quality standards for the deliverables.
- Communicating the above items to all employees.

Quality Control
Quality Control is product or service oriented and focuses on defect identification and detection. It is very often planned inspection, installed at the end of the line or process. Examples of Quality Control are:

- Final visual inspection for damage or scratches.
- Functional test on electronics.
- Testing software solutions.
- Management approval or signature on the final document.
- Applying Jidoka when problems occur [see section 6.8.3]

Quality Control activities are short term solutions to prevent the customer from defects. Although this is of course a very good initiative, all Quality Control measures mentioned above are classified as "Non-Value Added' or 'Waste' in terms of Lean Six Sigma. This is because the measures are not adding any value to a product. They only prevent a bad product will be delivered to the customer. The measures result in rework or scrap. Therefore Quality Control alone is not enough. Organizations should focus on prevention rather than detecting. This can be achieved by implementing Quality Assurance.

Quality Assurance
Quality Assurance is a way of preventing mistakes or defects in products and processes and ensuring continuous improvement. Quality Assurance is process oriented and focuses on defect prevention rather than defect identification. Quality assurance activities are to ensure that the process implemented to produce the product or service satisfy customer and legal requirements. It covers all activities from design, development, production, installation, servicing and documentation.

Two principles included in Quality Assurance are: 'Fit For Purpose', i.e. the product should be suitable for the intended purpose; and 'First Time Right' (FTR), i.e. mistakes and damage should be prevented, rather than repaired or inspected. Examples of Quality Assurance are:

- Applying Poka Yoke in product design.
- Composing a risk assessment before implementing a change.
- Validation and verification of software before release.
- Using formats.
- Execution of internal and external audits.

Whereas Quality Control is focused on inspection and blocking the release of defective products, Quality Assurance is focused on improving production and associated processes to avoid issues that led to the defects in the first place. However, Quality Assurance does not necessarily eliminate the need for Quality Control. Some product characteristics are so critical that inspection is still necessary just in case Quality Assurance fails.

4

4.3.2 Ongoing monitoring, evaluation and auditing

Ongoing monitoring, evaluation and auditing consists of two main components: ongoing risk assessment and ongoing control assessment. During ongoing risk assessments audit activities take place that identify and evaluate risks by examining current process performance trends compared to past performance or to the performance of a similar process elsewhere in the organization. While management is responsible for developing and maintaining a system that identifies and mitigates risk, auditors should assist the organization by identifying and evaluating significant exposures to risk.

During ongoing control assessment, audit activities take place that identify whether selected process controls are working properly. The audit procedures often are based on a sampling approach and include activities such as reviews of policies, procedures, approvals and reconciliations. A well-defined set of control rules warns organizations when processes or systems are not working as intended or are compromised.

Auditors should always be independent of the focus of the audit either by being part of an internal audit function or by being part of an external audit service. The practice of internal audit helps to maintain clear management support of the process controls currently in place and further helps by identifying opportunities for improvement. External audits equally support the same benefits as the internal audit function and additionally acts as third party independent assessment that can be used to maintain the confidence of customers and clients. Indeed in many sectors third party audit is a pre-requisite of doing business.

4

"The starting point for improvement

is to recognize the need."

- Masaaki Imai -

5
CIMM Process Level II
Creating a Continuous
Improvement culture

The second level is about creating a culture of proactive problem solving and Continuous Improvement activities. At this level we adhere to the Kaizen philosophy of Masaaki Imai. This is about creating a bottom-up approach with the objective that many small improvements will be executed by employees at the 'Gemba', rather than by top-down breakthrough improvement projects and change projects guided by project managers or management.

The idea behind this is that by realizing a large number of small improvements actually a big improvement has been made. This can be achieved by implementing short daily stand-up meetings with all people involved to discuss the daily output, the issues and agreement on the actions that need to be taken. The most commonly applied approach for problem solving at this level is the PDCA circle, which stands for Plan – Do – Check – Act. In this chapter we will also review a number of basic quality tools and brainstorming techniques that can be very helpful in Kaizen projects.

5.1 Kaizen

Kaizen reviews how to organize and facilitate improvement teams at the shop floor that work on improvement initiatives. The meaning of 'Kai' is change and the meaning of 'Zen' is meditation or contemplation. An explanation of the Japanese word Kaizen is: 'To disassemble and put together again in a better way'. The item that is disassembled is usually a process, a system, a product or a service. Masaaki Imai is the well-known founder of the Kaizen Institute Consulting Group. He wrote the books 'Kaizen' and 'Gemba Kaizen' [3.], meaning 'improving from the work-floor'.

5.1.1 Short Interval Management

Many organizations that implement Kaizen or Lean will also implement 'Lean Daily Management'. This is a system of organized periodic Stand-up meetings at the Gemba to review performance data, results and actions. The number of meetings depends on the type of work and on the situation, but should be held at least once a day.

Stand-up meetings are used to start the day as a team and to review progress during the day. The purpose is to keep the meeting short and to the point. Usually a meeting takes around 10 to 15 minutes and is held standing up, rather than sitting down with a cup of coffee. The location of the meeting is a fixed point in the work place that is arranged especially for this purpose with visual management boards. Some companies have located special corners with high tables to facilitate the stand-up meeting.

Figure 27 - Lean Daily Stand-up meeting

It is important that the information on the visual management board is accurate and reflects only the 'Key Performance Indicators' (KPIs) that are relevant to the people who attend the meeting. Furthermore the team should be able to influence the KPIs. If the team were to have no input, it would not make much sense to review the KPI. Typical data that is presented on the management boards is about the quantity and the quality of the department. Examples are the number of items produced, the number of requests processed, the amount of Work in Process, the average Lead Time, on time delivery, safety, the amount of rejects, the process yield, etc. It is not the intention that during each stand-up meeting all KPIs are reviewed. Up front it should be defined if certain KPIs should be reviewed daily, weekly or monthly.

5

'Short Interval Management' (SIM) is a bit more sophisticated. The SIM process engages team members to assess whether they are still on track to meet the established targets for the day. The term 'Short Interval' indicates that during the day at specified intervals the team's actual performance is compared to the planned performance for that interval. This action means that the team performance is checked regularly against the plan and reduces the response time if the team is underperforming and corrective actions are needed. The frequency of updates depends on the type of work and on the situation, but is about 2 to 4 times a day for about 5 to 15 minutes. Employees gather at a fixed time, following a fixed schedule:

Looking back - Review performance of the previous interval:

- Did we achieve the required quantity?
- Did we face any quality problems?
- Did we complete the actions that were defined in the prior interval?
- Were actions effective or are additional actions required?

Looking forward - Discuss the targets of the next interval:

- What are the required quantity and objectives?
- Do we have the necessary resources?
- Who will need help to meet their objectives?
- What specific actions are needed?

5

Figure 28 - *Short Interval Management*

Discipline is a very important element to guarantee successful stand-up meetings. People must arrive on time and the meeting should not wait for latecomers. Managers should lead by example, employees should come prepared and data should be accurate. Problems will not be solved during the meeting, but actions will be defined and assigned to people who will work to solve the problem. Results will be discussed during the next stand-up meeting. The meeting is not intended for extensive story telling or detailed reviewing activities. To keep meetings short and effective, each one should focus on facts and results rather than on guesses and excuses.

5.1.2 Visual Workplace

'Visual Workplace' is also known as 'Visual Factory', 'Visual Thinking' or 'Visual Management'. They all mean the same: making everything visible. Visual workplace helps operations to reduce waste and to maintain improvements over a long time. This is achieved by improving communication, by reducing complexity and by making abnormalities visible. Visualization is one of the key elements in Lean environments. Visualization of data by applying graphs is also a key element in Six Sigma.

A primary cause of mistakes and waste is missing information or miscommunication. Employees simply lack the information they need or communication between two persons is not clear. Employees may not fully understand priorities, deadlines or the proper way to perform tasks. This results in loss of time due to additional motion, searching, asking, waiting, retrieving, reworking and mistakes.

The purpose of a visual workplace is that everything is self-explanatory. Information about progress, priorities and quality is visible at a glance and at the point of use. This eliminates a lot of questions from employees to supervisors and department leaders. Lean also means an open communication. No problems are swept under the carpet, not even for suppliers and customers who visit the shop floor.

Real time information, clear instructions, expectations (goals), visual aids, warning signals, standards operating instructions and other critical operations knowledge help employees to know what to do, when to do and how to do it. Visual workplace plays a very important role in creating an empowered workforce and Continuous Improvement culture that is key in any Kaizen and Lean transformation process.

Figure 29 - *Visual workplace*

Examples of visual workplace are listed below. Within this book you will find several examples. Also many examples can be found on the internet.

- 5S programs and 5S red tags.
- Short interval control boards.
- Communication and status boards.
- Shadow boards for tooling (SMED) [see section 6.6.3].
- Floor marking, identification of aisles, areas and equipment.
- White walls, white floors, white machines and white lab coats (to identify abnormalities).
- Identifying storage areas for work in process.
- Color-coding and labeling of tools and work in process.
- Plasticizing procedures.
- Andon lights to visualize equipment status [see section 6.8.3].
- Kanban racks and Kanban cards [see section 6.6.1].
- Visual reorder indicators.
- Visual displays such as scoreboards for quality, on-time delivery and safety [see section 5.1.1].
- Visual displays with pictures of employees and recognition displays.
- Poka Yoke [see section 6.8.3].

5.1.3 Root Cause Analysis (RCA)

'Root Cause Analysis' (RCA) is a method of problem solving that tries to identify the root causes of faults or problems. RCA arose in the 1950s as a formal study following the introduction of Kepner-Tregoe Analysis. There are many different approaches for performing RCA though, containing different techniques such as 5-Whys, Is-Is Not and the Cause & Effect diagram. RCA is typically applied after an event has occurred as a reactive method of identifying and eliminating root causes.

Using the correct terminology is necessary within RCA to prevent confusion. The following list of definitions will help to ensure clarity.

Figure 30 - *Symptom versus Root Cause*

- Symptom: A characteristic or complaint belonging to a specific problem
- Effect: A deviation of expectation (Problem) or unexpected effect with unknown cause(s).
- Failure: The way in which a component fails functionally, causing a problem.
- Cause: The contributing factors that led to the failure.
- Root Cause: The deepest underlying reason for the cause to originate.

A number of examples are listed in Table 5.1.:

Table 5.1. *Examples Root Cause Analysis*

Symptom	Effect	Failure	Cause	Root Cause
Poor readability document	Copier gives vague print	Not enough toner	Empty toner	No procedure to replace toner in time
Room is dark	No light in the room	Defective bulb	Broken tungsten wire	Tungsten wire worn out over time
Not able to drive a car	Engine won't start	No battery power	Empty battery	Battery not replaced during maintenance
High absenteeism	Sick employee	Overworked employee	High workload	No proper resource planning

In this section we will discuss two approaches to solve issues and to improve performance: Kaizen and Problem Solving Process (sometimes called the 8D process). To support the improvement activities a number of Basic quality tools and Brainstorm tools will be explained.

5.1.4 Kaizen Events

Kaizen focuses on Continuous Improvement. A Kaizen Event is typically about a small improvement project, like waste elimination and Cycle Time reduction. Examples of Kaizen events are:

- Improve equipment set up and tooling change.
- Improving ergonomics and safety.
- Improving quality.
- Reduction of cost.
- Designing bins and racks for storage of raw components and finished goods.
- Designing forms, templates and inspection criteria.
- Waste identification and elimination.
- Problem solving activities to prevent quality issues.

Kaizen is about teamwork and empowerment. Participation is voluntary, but not without commitment. It is a bottom-up approach and encourages the involvement of all employees. As such, Kaizen is an approach that is often used to create a culture of Continuous Improvement. Kaizen is carried out at the place where it happens: the 'Gemba'. When problems occur you should 'Go to the Gemba' rather than looking for solutions behind a desk or in a meeting room. Problems on the shop floor are experienced mostly by employees on the shop floor, rather than by managers sitting behind spreadsheets and PowerPoints. Employees on the shop floor very often have good ideas for solutions and improvements. The only issue is that managers forget to ask them and involve them.

The five foundations of Kaizen are listed in Table 5.2.:

Table 5.2. *Kaizen principles*

Kaizen principle	Description
Teamwork	Create commitment for all
Personal discipline	Follow the standards
Better moral	Ensure good work morale
The quality circle	Follow the PDCA improvement cycles
Suggestion for improvement	Be receptive to new ideas and suggestions

Kaizen events are coupled very often to Standardized Work, as discussed in section [4.2]. If an abnormality occurs, always ask yourself the following: 'Was there no standard?', 'Was the standard followed?', 'Was the standard insufficient?'

The customer should always be the starting point of improvement projects. This not only concerns the external customer, but also the internal customer (e.g. colleagues and departments). Each step in the process has a customer who receives the outcome of its process step. At the same time each process step is a customer itself, as it receives products from the prior process step. Therefore it is important that each process step is treated like a customer. Each process step should not accept errors from prior steps; it should not make errors and it should not forward errors to consecutive process steps. If everybody follows this principle, the quality of the entire process will be better and at the end of the process the customer will receive a good product or service.

A Kaizen event is about getting things done immediately, not about making weeks of analysis and then taking a few more weeks to implement the solution. The solution will not always be perfect after the first event, but a big improvement will be made. Later on, we can start another event and make another step.

"Better to be 80% right today
than 100% right in six months!"

5

A typical kaizen event is the Kaizen Blitz. It is the most well known and most effective way of achieving immediate and obvious gains within any environment (service or manufacturing). The Kaizen Blitz event takes a few days to a week and is led by a facilitator (e.g. Lean facilitator, supervisor or external consultant). The team focuses on one specific area. Typically a Kaizen Blitz concentrates on the removal of the eight types of 'Waste'. We will discuss these types in section [6.4]. The first Kaizen Blitz can be very much like an initial 5S implementation, looking at work cell design, layout and safety. The strength of any Kaizen approach is gaining the result within a short period of time.

Genchi Genbutsu
'Genchi Genbutsu' means "Go and See". It is one of the principles of the Toyota Production System. It means that in order to truly understand a situation one needs to go to Gemba or Genba, as the Japanese call it. 'Gen' means actuality or reality. When we look at the word Gen-Ba, it means the actual place or the place where the work is done.

Taiichi Ohno, creator of the Toyota Production System, had a special way of teaching managers the power of Genchi Genbutsu. He drew a circle on the shop floor with a piece of chalk. The manager would be told to stand in the circle, observe and note what he saw. Several hours later, Ohno would return and ask the manager "What did you see?". Usually Ohno had spotted an irregularity, and wanted the manager to see the same. So if the manager's reply was something else than what Ohno had already seen, his response would be "Watch some more". The chalk circle is therefore also called the 'Ohno Circle'.

Ohno's statement was that the only way to truly understand what happens on the shop floor was to go there and observe. He truly believed that value is created at the shop floor only, and also problems should be solved on the shop floor. Therefore the shop floor is where managers should spend their time.

5.2 Basic Quality tools

There are a number of graphical tools that have been identified as helpful in troubleshooting quality issues. These tools are called the 'Basic Quality tools' and 'Basic Management tools'. They are called 'Basic' because they are suitable for people with little formal training in statistics and because they can be used to solve many quality issues. Therefore, these tools are very often used in Kaizen initiatives. These tools and techniques stand in contrast to more advanced statistical methods and Six Sigma tools, that will be discussed in sequel chapters.

5.2.1 Visualization of data

Converting data into a visual representation is very powerful in problem solving activities. People cannot be expected to interpret a set of raw data like a computer. However people are very good in interpreting images and graphs. You will find that making a graphical representation of a problem will be a very powerful tool in explaining the situation and discussing the possible solutions.

Visualization of data has two key purposes. The first is to help us in graphical data analysis to develop hypotheses regarding trends, groups and correlations within the data. These hypotheses can then lead to further data collection and testing with a view to drawing a statistically valid conclusion. The second use of visualization of data is then used to communicate findings and conclusions to others.

Excellence in visualization of data includes complex ideas communicated with clarity, precision and efficiency and should:

- show the data;
- induce the viewer to think about the substance rather than something else;
- avoid distorting what the data have to say;
- present many numbers in a small space;
- make large data sets coherent;
- encourage the eye to compare different pieces of data;
- reveal the data at several levels of detail, from a broad overview to the fine structure;
- serve a reasonably clear purpose: description, exploration, tabulation or decoration;
- be closely integrated with the statistical and verbal descriptions of a data set.

Source: 'The Visual Display of Quantitative Information', (Edward Tufte, 1983).

5.2.2 Basic Quality tools

In this paragraph we will review commonly used visualizations. Most of these tools are part of the so called 'Basic Quality tools'. These tools can be very useful in Kaizen initiatives. Some of the graphical tools will be demonstrated, using Minitab. However, most of these tools can also be applied using Excel or even pen and paper. In the next sections we will discuss the following Quality tools:

1. Check sheet
2. Pareto chart
3. Scatter plot
4. Bar chart
5. Pie chart
6. Time Series plot
7. Histogram
8. Box plot

1 - Check sheet

A Check sheet (or Tally sheet) is a tool to collect data at the location where the data is generated. This can be a machine or a desk location in the office. It is the intention to collect real time data. The purpose of a check sheet is to collect data on a sheet instead of entering these in a computer or system. The defining characteristic of a check sheet is that data is recorded by making marks ('checks') to visualize the data.

Examples of a check sheet can be the recording of the number of defects on a product or the number of phone calls by a call center.

Tally sheet				
Lamp defect	|||			
Illegible code	ЦII	ЦII	II		
Empty battery	ЦII	ЦII	ЦII	I	
Scratch on lens	II				
Broken ring	ЦII	II			
Missing cord	ЦII				

Figure 31 - *Check sheet*

2 - Pareto chart

The Pareto chart is a type of chart that contains both bars and a line graph. Individual values are represented by bars. The chart is named after Vilfredo Pareto. The purpose of the Pareto chart is to highlight the single most important factor among a (typically large) set of factors. In quality control, it often represents the most common sources of defects, the highest occurring type of defect, or the most frequent reasons for customers to complain, and so on.

The first difference between a normal bar chart and a Pareto chart is that the bars are presented in descending order. The left vertical axis is the frequency of occurrence, but it can alternatively represent cost or another important unit of measure. The second difference is that it shows a second vertical axis on the right. This axis is the cumulative percentage of the total number of occurrences, total cost or total of the particular unit of measure. Because the bars are in a decreasing height order, the cumulative function is a concave function. Figure 32 demonstrates the causes for late deliveries of packages. Lowering the amount of late deliveries by almost 84% can be achieved by solving the first three issues. The Pareto chart is the graphical representation of the well-known 80%-20% rule.

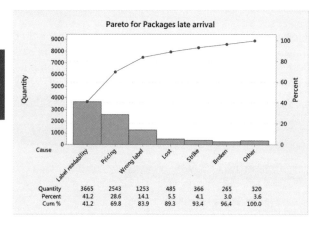

Figure 32 - *Pareto chart*

3 - Scatter plot

The scatter plot is used to study the potential relationship between two continuous variables. This is done by drawing each variable on a different axis. In the graph we can see the relation between the water usage and electric charges of homes.

As you can see there seems to be a relation that shows that families who use more water, also have higher charges for electric. If the measurements on the graph would look like a cloud of points, there is no relation.

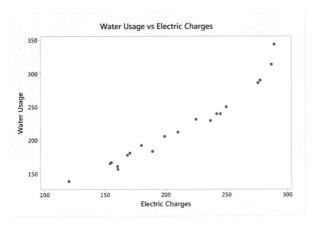

Figure 33 - *Scatter plot*

Scatterplots are also useful for plotting a variable over time. Unlike a Time series plot, you must provide a time variable from the worksheet yourself. This is especially useful for data that are not entered in chronological order or were collected at irregular intervals.

4 - Bar chart

Bar charts are used to visually compare category measures like quantities or frequencies for two or more groups. There are several different variants of charts. Different types of Bar charts can be made with software like Excel or Minitab. A few possible variants of Bar charts are shown below:

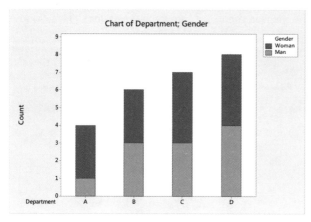

Counts of unique values:
Use this Bar chart if you have one or more columns of categorical data and you want to chart the frequency of each category.

Figure 34 - *Bar chart*

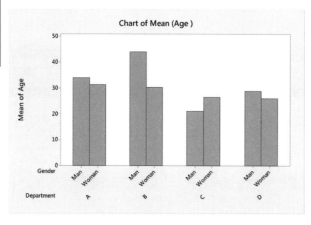

A function of a variable:
Use this Bar chart if you have one or more columns of quantitative data and you want to chart a function of the measurement data, such as gender.

Figure 35 - *Bar chart*

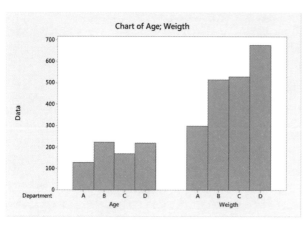

Values from a table:
Use this Bar chart if you have one or more columns of summary data and you want to chart the summary value for each category.

Figure 36 - *Bar chart*

5 - Pie chart

A Pie chart visually represents the proportion of different categories. The pie is divided into slices, with each slice representing a category. By comparing and contrasting the size of the slices, you can evaluate the relative magnitude of each category.

For example, a hospital collects data from patients to find the most common causes of no-shows for appointments. A pie chart with five slices is presented. Each slice displays a common cause of 'No Show' and the frequency of the data.

Reason	Quantity
Forgot appointment	65
Got sick	3
No more complaints	45
Too busy	25
No reason	32

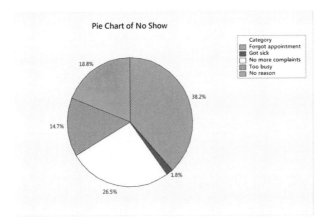

Figure 37 - *Pie chart*

6 - Time Series plot

The Time Series plot is a very simple tool. Yet, together with the Histogram, it is one of the most powerful tools of Six Sigma. Time Series plots can help you to observe (sudden) changes and trends over time, which cannot be observed by Histograms.

On the horizontal axis the time is plotted, while on the vertical axis a performance measure is plotted. This measure is very often the measure that is related to the problem focus of the project (e.g. dimension, temperature, amount of defects, Lead Time). As soon as the first data are collected this is often one of the first graphs that is plotted after the start of a new project. It gives the team an indication of the extend of the problem over a certain period of time.

Examples of behavior that can be observed within Time Series plot are:

- Upwards or downwards trends (fig. A).
- Amount of variation and changes in variation (fig. B).
- Structural bad performance or defects caused by outliers (fig. C).
- Sudden changes in measurement or performance (fig. D).
- Difference between short time performance and long time performance.
- Patterns or cycles in performance.

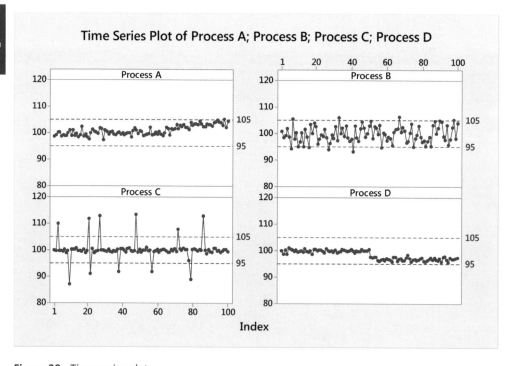

Figure 38 - Time series plots

7 - Histogram

Histograms are used to divide sample values into a certain number of intervals. These intervals are called 'bins' and are represented by bars. Each bar represents the number of observations (or frequency) falling within one bin. Histograms are used to examine the shape and spread of data. The histogram in figure 39 demonstrates 8 bins on the x-axis. Each bin represents a certain amount of water usage. On the y-axis the number of families who have water usage that fall is represented within each bin.

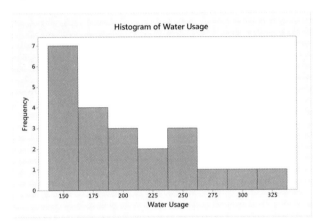

Figure 39 - *Histogram*

When more data are available, it may make sense to draw a probability density function over the histogram in order to make a visual evaluation of the shape of the distribution of the data. Figure 40 depicts a histogram with a normal probability density function drawn over it. Green and Black Belts are expected to perform several types of calculation on histograms, while Yellow and Orange Belts are expected to understand and interpret the graphical representation of a histogram.

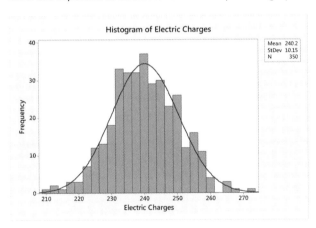

Figure 40 - *Histogram*

8 - Box plot

A Box plot (also called 'Box-and-whisker plot') gives a graphical summary of the distribution of a sample that shows its shape, central tendency, and variability. The Box plot consists of the following elements:

- Q_0 = Lowest value of the data
- Q_1 = Lower Quartile
- Q_2 = Median
- Q_3 = Upper Quartile
- Q_4 = Highest value

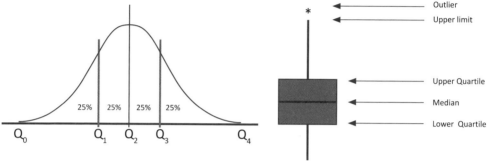

Figure 41 - *Box plot versus normal distribution*

Median calculation:
The Median can be found by arranging the data in ascending order and choosing the middle value. So for data {5,9,1,7,4} arranged in ascending order {1,4,5,7,9}, the middle value is 5 and so is the Median. If there is an even number of values then we take the arithmetic Mean of the two middle values. So for data {2,9,1,7,6,8} arranged in ascending order {1,2,6,7,8,9}, the middle values are 6 and 7 and the Median is 6.5.

Quartile calculation:
There are various methods of finding the value of the Quartiles. One possibility is to use the excel function QUARTILE.EXC to calculate Quartiles.
Q1: 'First Quartile' or 'Lower Quartile':   25% of the data are less than or equal to this value.
Q2: 'Second Quartile' or 'Median':   50% of the data are less than or equal to this value.
Q3: 'Third Quartile' or 'Upper Quartile':   75% of the data are less than or equal to this value.

So for data {1,9,7,3,4,6,1,8,6} arranged into order {1,1,3,4,6,6,7,8,9}, the Median of all the data is the first 6 which splits the data set into a lower half {1,1,3,4} and an upper half {6,7,8,9}. The Lower Quartile Q1 is the median of the lower half data {1,1,3,4} and is 2. The Upper Quartile Q3 is the median of the upper half data {6,7,8,9} and is 7.5. In the event that there are an even number of values in the main dataset then simply split them into the upper half and lower half for the quartile calculation.

Box plots are particularly useful for comparing distributions between several groups or sets of data, because it is very easy to plot several Box plots in one graph. With histograms this is not possible, because it would look confusing. Figure 42 demonstrates that process C has many outliers, while process D has the lowest Median.

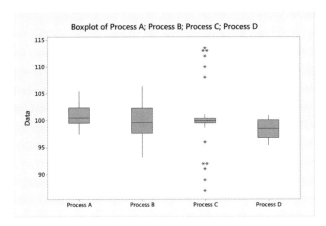

Figure 42 - *Box plot*

5.3 Basic Management tools

In this section we will review a few management tools that are very powerful in the problem solving process. These tools apply brainstorming within the team. During the brainstorming process criticism of ideas is not allowed. 'Out-of-the-box' thinking is important to generate as many ideas as possible. Causes or ideas need not necessarily supported by data or facts. Brainstorming is an idea generation process. Verification will be done later on.

5.3.1 Brainstorm techniques

Brainstorm techniques are creative processes used by teams to produce lots of possible ideas (the trivial many) in response to a single question or statement prior to then prioritizing the most likely results (the trivial few). Brainstorming can be used at many different stages in the process improvement project: to develop ideas for CTQs; to identify helpful measures; to record all the potential causes or to generate lots of possible solutions.

It is advisable to facilitate the brainstorming in two phases: an opening phase of silent individual brainstorming reduces the likelihood of a dominant or senior member of the team inadvertently leading the team down a single train of thought (group think); a summarizing stage that involves the whole team can then be used to share, capture and group the ideas and simultaneously encourage the synergetic process that produces innovative spin off ideas.

Three common brainstorm techniques are:

1. Affinity diagram
2. 5-Whys method
3. Cause & Effect diagram (Ishikawa)

1 - Affinity diagram

The Affinity diagram is a brainstorm tool used to organize causes or ideas. It is one of the Basic Management and Planning Tools. The technique name 'Affinity diagram' was devised by Kawakita in the 1960s.

The technique is often used within problem solving projects to create an overview after a brainstorm session about possible root causes or improvement suggestions. This is done by clustering items that are similar or can be combined in a certain way. The best results will be achieved when the session is performed by a cross-functional team.

In a problem solving session the Affinity diagram follows these steps:

1. Each team member receives a bundle of post-Its.
2. Each team member writes suspected causes on post-Its.
3. The causes will be pasted on the wall.
4. Post-Its will be sorted into clusters when they are related or similar.
5. Common headlines will be defined for each cluster.

Sometimes headlines will be defined before the brainstorm session starts (step 5 will be put after step 1).

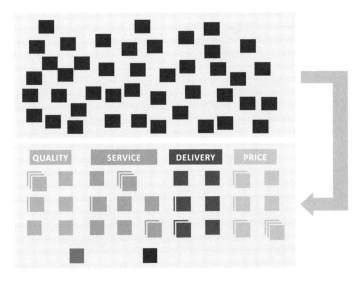

Figure 43 - *Affinity diagram*

2 - 5-Whys method

The 5-Whys is an iterative question-asking technique used to explore the Cause-and-Effect relationships underlying a particular problem. The primary goal of the technique is to determine the root cause of a defect or problem. The technique was originally developed by Sakichi Toyoda and incorporated in the Toyota Production System. Today the 5-Whys has seen widespread use beyond Toyota. It is used within Kaizen, 8D problem solving (step D4), Lean manufacturing and Six Sigma improvement programs.

The 5-Whys has to answer three questions which are visualized in a 'Tree diagram':

A. Why did the problem occur?
B. Why was it only detected at the client?
C. Why did the 'System' not function?

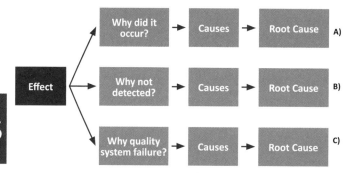

Figure 44 - *5-Whys Tree diagram*

---

1. Why did the machine stop during production?
   → The drive chain is broken.
2. Why is the drive chain broken?
   → The bearings have been broken.
3. Why are the bearings broken?
   → The bearings have run dry.
4. Why are the bearings run dry?
   → The lubricating oil pipe to the bearings is broken.
5. Why is the lubricating oil pipe broken?
   → A pallet truck has hit the lubricating oil pipe.
6. Why did the pallet truck hit the lubricating oil pipe?
   → The oil pipeline runs unprotected outside the machine.

   Solution: Move the lubricating oil pipe or place a guardrail.

Figure 45 - *Example 5-Whys*

3 - Ishikawa diagram

The purpose of the Ishikawa diagram is to collect possible Causes for a certain Effect by conducting a brainstorm session. In most cases the Effect is a failure mode or problem statement. Kaoru Ishikawa (1968) created this type of graphical visualization. The Ishikawa diagram is also known as the Fishbone or Cause & Effect diagram. Fishbone refers to the graphical shape of the diagram, because it looks like a fish.

Causes can be derived by performing a brainstorming session with a group of people. The outcome of this brainstorm session is often enlightening but also depends very much on the people who participate in the session. To facilitate the thinking process of the attendees six major groups of causes have been determined. These are called the 6 Ms. The group should focus on one M at a time to identify as many as possible potential causes within that group.

1. Manufacturing: Technology or equipment related causes.
2. Method: Process related causes.
3. Material: Raw Material or information
4. Man: Causes related to people or employees.
5. Measurement: Causes related to measurement tools or inspection methods.
6. Mother Nature: Environmental causes.

In the first phase of the brainstorm session as many potential causes as possible per major group will be collected. Of course not all these potential causes will be the actual or significant causes of the effect. Therefore a second round is needed to group causes and to highlight the causes that are highly suspected. At the end of this second round the result should be a limited number of potential causes that need further investigation.

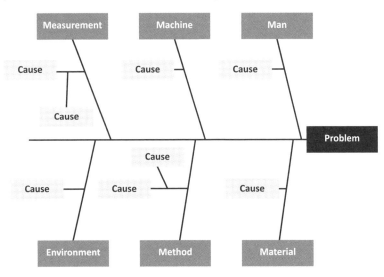

Figure 46 - *Ishikawa diagram*

5.3.2 Decision making

When working on process improvement projects, making the right decisions can lead to success, while making the wrong decisions can result to failure. Therefore it is important that thoughtful consideration is put into each decision that needs to be made. Visualization of data and brainstorm techniques, as reviewed in the previous sections, support the decision making process. In this section we will list some other techniques and tools that can be used to make decisions. The basic principles of these tools are similar though. The steps to be followed are about identifying the decision to be made, gathering relevant information, weighting evidence and finally choosing the best alternative.

The 'Cause & Effect matrix' (C&E matrix) is a tool that is used to focus on the most important factors of influence. It shows the strength and relationship between the factors of influence (Causes) and Responses (Results or Effects). It connects the process input variables to the process output variables.

- Step 1: Enter the output variables or effects (Key Process Output variables – KPOV).
- Step 2: Enter the specifications of the outputs or requirements (from the CTQ-Tree).
- Step 3: Indicate the importance of each output for the customer or for the organization (1 to 10).
- Step 4: Enter the factors of influence or causes (Key Process Input variables – KPIV).
- Step 5: Define the correlation between the Inputs and the Outputs.
- Step 6: Calculate the total score for each KPIV.

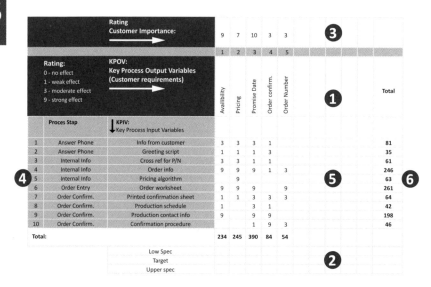

Figure 47 - *Cause & Effect matrix*

5

"The most dangerous kind of waste is

the waste we do not recognize."

- Shigeo Shingo -

6

CIMM Process Level III Creating stable and efficient processes

During the first two Continuous Improvement maturity levels the workplace has been organized, standards have been determined and a system has been put in place to solve problems and to continuously work on improving the operation. The third maturity level focuses on improving the logistical flow and making it stable, efficient and predictable. The main objective of creating stable processes is intended to avoid incidents, stress, fire-fighting, downtime, unsafe situations, quality slips, mistakes etc. In other words the creation of an environment where you can predict what will happen and what can be promised to the client.

In this chapter we will review tools to visualize and analyze the process flow. We will review how to identify waste and opportunities for improvement. Also we will review a number of tools and techniques that are very powerful for improving efficiency, effectiveness, productivity and agility. We will review the five principles of Lean and Value Stream Mapping, which are amongst the most powerful tools for this level. Finally we will review how to eliminate Muda (Waste), Muri (Overburden) and Mura (Unevenness).

6

A number of tools that can be used at this CIMM-level are presented in Table 6.1. It is important to realize that it is not necessary to use each of these tools in your project. The table only demonstrates tools that are commonly used. Other tools can be used as well. It is also important to realize that not each tool mentioned in this table is expected to be applied by Yellow and Orange Belts. Some tools are only applied at the level of Green and Black Belt.

The roadmap used in this level is the DMAIC roadmap, which stands for Define, Measure, Analyze, Improve and Control. Although the origin of this roadmap is from Six Sigma, it can be followed in Lean projects as well. The tools listed in Table 6.1 are placed in one the DMAIC phases. However, many tools they can be used in other phases as well.

Table 6.1. Optional tools Level III

Define	Measure	Analyze	Improve	Control
Project Charter	Performance Metrics	VSM - Current State	VSM - Future State	Standardized Work
Voice of Customer	Time Series Plot	Graphical Tools	Kaizen improvements	5S
Costs of Poor Quality	OEE Analysis	Ishikawa	Reducing Muda (8 x Waste)	First Time Right, Poka Yoke
SIPOC		Brainstorm Techniques	Reducing Muri (Overburden)	Jidoka
Process Mapping		Affinity Diagram	Flow, Balancing, TOC	Visual Management
Swimlane			Reducing Mura (Unevenness)	Performance Management
Pareto			Pull, Kanban, FIFO, CONWIP	Short Interval Management
CTQ Flowdown			Leveling	FMEA, Control Plan
Stakeholder Analysis			SMED	Standard Operation Procedure
				Training (Skill development)
				Maintenance (TPM)
				Statistical Process Control
				Auditing

6

Define

6.1 Process Mapping

A process is a systematic series of activities that are required to achieve a goal. The series of activities uses one or more types of input and creates outputs with added value for the customer. Charting the process in a visual representation will work like a map to guide the team. Discussions about scope, objectives and causes will be visualized by pointing out places on the map and by drawing lines and by making notes on the map.

Figure 48 - *Process model*

There are different ways of mapping a process. In this section we will discuss different tools that are often used in both Lean and Six Sigma projects.

6

6.1.1 Process Flow Diagram

A Process Map – or Flow Chart or 'Process Flow Diagram' (PFD) – is a diagram commonly used to indicate the general flow of activities carried out on the product and of decisions to be made. A process flow is also a graphical representation of the routing of the product. In 'Process thinking' it is important to understand what happens in the company and to understand how the work is done. Mapping the process is a way to instruct employees of what to do in a graphical way rather than a written description. It is also a way to identify and reduce Waste in the process. Process Maps can be used:

- to communicate the processes;
- to define the scope of a project;
- to describe and understand the processes;
- to document and standardize the processes;
- to define responsibilities and competencies;
- to analyze the processes / problems;
- to identify improvement opportunities.

There are different ways to map a process. The SIPOC explained in section [6.1.2] is one way of mapping the process. A schematic representation of a Pizzeria process is demonstrated in Figure 49. This example is from the perspective of the Pizza Chef. It has a clear start (Take order) and end (Deliver); it has a number of process steps (Activities) and a decision point (Inspection).

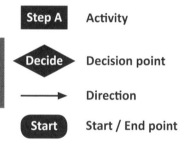

Figure 49 - *Most common symbols*

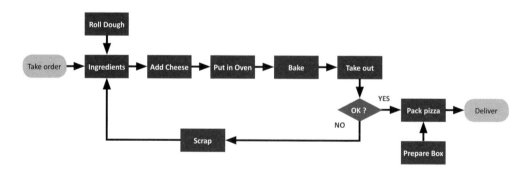

Figure 50 - *Process Flow diagram*

6.1.2 High level process description

In this section we will review two tools that can be used for describing the process at a high level. The first tool is the Spaghetti diagram and the second tool is the SIPOC. The Spaghetti diagram is often used in Lean projects, while the SIPOC is often used in Six Sigma projects.

Spaghetti diagram

A Spaghetti diagram is used to track the routing on the shop floor. Spaghetti plots visualize movement and transportation of a product or document. Analyzing flows through systems can determine where time and energy is wasted, and identifies where streamlining would be beneficial.

The tool is not only used for physical products, but also for more abstract products like a passport or request for a car insurance. If you visualize for the first time all the movements of a product before it is finished, you will probably be amazed. Analyzing the movements and transportations will determine the amount of time that is wasted and identifies where streamlining would be valuable.

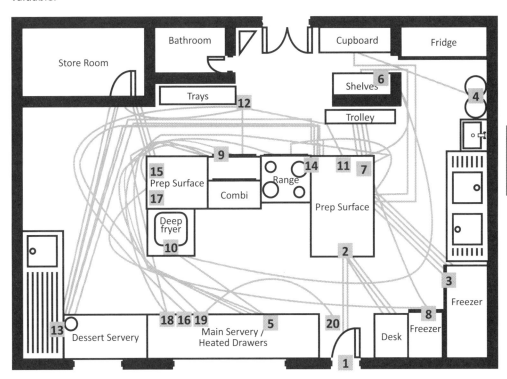

Figure 51 - *Spaghetti diagram*

SIPOC

A SIPOC analysis is one of the first steps in a Six Sigma improvement project. The acronym SIPOC stands for Suppliers, Inputs, Process, Outputs and Customers. It is a high-level process description that defines the scope of the process, the main inputs, outputs, customers and suppliers. Creating a SIPOC can be done in the Define phase or Measure phase. Detailed process mapping however should be avoided in this phase of the project. This will be done later in the Analyze phase. SIPOC is also very helpful before performing a full and detailed Value Stream Map.

SIPOC helps with:

- A high level Process description   P
- Identification of Suppliers and Customers   S/C
- Identification of Inputs and Outputs   I/O

The entire process from supplier to customer can be very long and focus is needed to be effective in finding the root cause and solving the problem. The SIPOC helps you to determine which phase of the process needs analysis and improvement effort. It also helps to make a rough distinction between the dependent and independent factors of influence and to compose a list of input and output variables to investigate.

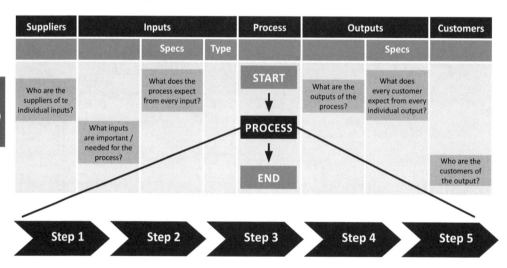

Figure 52 - *SIPOC*

SIPOC is a team effort. The team composition should be such that it contains people with different functions related to the process to assure that all suppliers, customers, activities, inputs and outputs are included. It regularly involves people from the Yellow Belt to Black Belt level. Creating a SIPOC is an iterative process. You can start with the complaint of the client, with the fall-out in the process itself or with the supplier who is causing the problem.

The result of creating a SIPOC with the team is to compose a visual map of all elements that are related to the complaint or problem. In the end the team will better understand the relations between the elements and will be able to highlight elements that need further analysis or investigation in the next phase.

Steps for creating a SIPOC:

- Customers:
  List the client who is experiencing the problem. Also enter a list of clients who have obtained the same product or service, but did not encounter the problem or did not complain. Instead of external clients, we can also start here with an internal process that has a low yield.

- Outputs:
  Enter a list of outputs. These are measures of the process (CTQ_{int}). Clients can be coupled to process outputs, requirements or specifications. It is not necessary to determine a client for each output.

- Process:
  Compose a high level overview of the process (vertical), mentioning the start and the end of the process The key process step(s) that are linked to the problem, are expanded at the bottom of the SIPOC (horizontal) in 4 to max. 7 steps. It is not the intention to apply more detail at this stage.

- Inputs:
  Enter a list of inputs that are needed for the process. If specifications have been defined for a certain input, it should be listed in the 'Specs' column. Optionally you can list the Input type (Controllable, Noise or Standard Operating Procedure).

- Suppliers:
  Enter a list of suppliers to the process. Suppliers can be coupled to an Input description or a requirement. It is not necessary to determine a supplier for each Input.

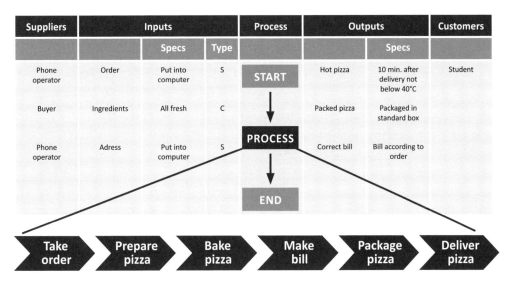

Figure 53 - *SIPOC*

Measure

6.2 Lean performance metrics

In this paragraph we will review how to analyze the process flow and we will review metrics that are used to determine how well the operational process is running, which is an important element in Operations Management.

Operations Management is concerned with managing the process that converts inputs (e.g. raw materials, resources) into outputs (goods or services). Operations management programs include manufacturing and production management, equipment maintenance management, resource management, process and systems analysis, productivity analysis and cost control, and materials planning.

6.2.1 Process Flow Analysis

In the era of the Industrial revolution, many manufacturing operations invested in expensive equipment. It was important to get the most out of each equipment. The goal was to Increase utilization on equipment. Utilization is defined as the proportion of the available time that a piece of equipment or a system is operating. It is necessary though to break through the conceptual barrier of throughput thinking and leave utilization thinking behind, as it will lead to excessive work in process which is not in line with Lean concepts. Teams that are working on Continuous Improvement initiatives in a Lean environment should focus on effectiveness, efficiency, productivity and agility instead.

Little's law

A measure that represents the efficiency of a process is the average Lead Time. This is the average time of one product or service passing through the entire process. Average Lead Time can be calculated by using the formula developed by Little (1954), also called 'Little's Law':

$$Average\ Lead\ Time = \frac{Work\ in\ Process}{Completion\ Rate}$$

The WIP level is the amount of work (e.g. orders, products) that is waiting on the shop floor or in the process. The Completion rate is the number of products or services that are completed in a specific time period (e.g. per minute, hour or day). This is also called the 'Output' of the process.

The formula developed by Little shows that the average Lead Time is constant if the WIP-level is constant. A constant Lead Time will make an operation predictable, which is more important than being fast. It also shows that WIP is a major cause of long Lead Times and that reducing WIP is one of the best ways of achieving a faster process.

Example: if you have 100 requests for a new passport waiting on your desk and you can complete 5 requests per hour, the average Lead Time is 20 hours.

$$Average\ Lead\ Time = \frac{Work\ in\ Process}{Completion\ Rate} = \frac{100\ requests}{5\ requests\ per\ hour} = 20\ hours$$

6.2.2 Lean performance metrics

One of the core principles of process improvement is that management should be based on facts. Hence, reliable and accurate data are required. Like with all other processes the collection of data is also a process, which should be managed appropriately. In practice it has been proven to be difficult to explain to a person what data are needed and how it should be collected. The Team should make sure that the measurement system and data are valid and reliable before it continues with analyzing it. It is therefore important to spend sufficient time in order to agree on the definitions of the project objective and the associated measurable target. This includes good definitions and identification of the sources and systems to extract the data from.

Process performance measures are important to sustain and improve performance. Performance metrics need to be measured over time to ensure that performance will not deteriorate. 'Key Performance Indicators' (KPIs) are used to classify the performance against a maximum (e.g. 96% of the products are ok) or against a certain goal (e.g. 92% of the deliveries arrived within 48 hours). Typical KPIs in Lean projects are 'On Time Delivery' (OTD); 'Net Promoter Score' (NPS); 'Overall Equipment Effectiveness' (OEE); 'Costs of Poor Quality' (COPQ) and number of defects. Typical Six Sigma measures are related to quality e.g. 'parts per million' (ppm), 'Defects Per Million Opportunities' (DPMO), 'Defects Per Unit' (DPU), 'Process Capability' (Cpk) and 'Rolled Throughput Yield '(RTY). In this section we will review the metrics that are more related to Lean projects, while in paragraph 7.2 we will review the metrics that are more related to Six Sigma projects. In the next sections we will also review the following metrics:

- Takt Time:
  The rhythm at which products are requested by the customer (or market).
- Cycle Time:
  The (average) time between the completions of two successive products or the time it takes an employee to go through all of the work elements before repeating them.
- Lead Time:
  The time for a product or service to travel the entire process from start to finish.
- Work in Process (WIP):
  The number of products or amount of Work in Process or waiting.
- Yield loss:
  The amount of products not meeting customer requirements.
- Overall Equipment Effectiveness (OEE):
  The measure that represents the effectiveness of a line, machine or plant.

Takt Time

The rhythm at which products are requested by the customer (or market). It is defined by the customer, and not by the process or by the planning department. It can be calculated by dividing the 'Available work time' by the 'Customer demand'. In 'Theory of Constraints' (TOC) this measure is called the 'Drumbeat of the process'.

$$Takt\ Time = \frac{Available\ Work\ Time}{Customer\ Demand}$$

Figure 54 - *Takt Time*

Cycle Time

This is the average time between completion of two consecutive products. Cycle time should not be confused with processing time of a particular process step. For example, if three people perform a specific process step in parallel, the Cycle time is one-third of the processing time.

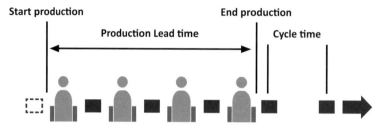

Figure 55 - *Cycle Time*

Lead Time

The lead time is the sum of all processing times and waiting times. For the organization itself, the Lead time is the average time between the start of the production of a new product and the completion of the same product. However, from the customer's perspective, the Lead time starts with submitting a sales order, or request, and ends at the time the order is delivered or service is completed.

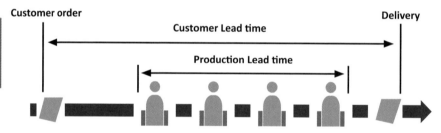

Figure 56 - *Lead Time*

Overall Equipment Effectiveness (OEE)

A measure developed by Seiichi Nakajima in the 1960s to evaluate how effectively a manufacturing operation is utilized. It is a measure used in Total Productive Maintenance programs. It is also commonly used as a Key Performance Indicator in conjunction with Lean Manufacturing programs in heavily machine oriented industries like food and automotive. When it is too complicated to measure the OEE on all equipment, it should at least be done on bottleneck operations to manage the efficiency and effectiveness of the bottleneck of the plant. The OEE measure is the mathematical product of three elements: Availability, Performance and Quality:

$$OEE = (Availability[\%]) \times (Performance[\%]) \times (Quality[\%])$$

6.2.3 Data types

Before you gather information about the properties of a process or service, you must realize that there are different types of data. Data can be divided into two groups: Qualitative or Quantitative. Qualitative data are descriptive information and describe properties. Quantitative data are numerical information and can be measured or counted. Applying statistical methods is more valuable for quantitative measures than for qualitative measures.

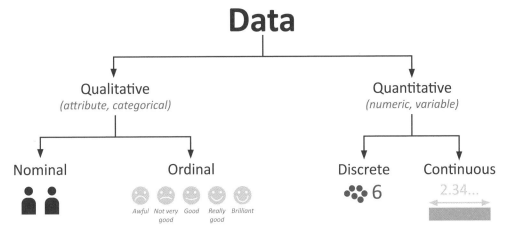

Figure 57 - *Qualitative data versus Quantitative data*

1 - Qualitative data:
Qualitative data cannot actually be measured. As you know 'There is no arguing about matters of taste'. It is not possible to measure 'taste' like the length of a bar can be measured for instance. You can qualify this type of data by assigning a characteristic or property to the object. These properties of an object are called attributes. For example 'taste' can be qualified as 'It tasted good', or 'it tasted bad'. Other examples are the attributes of a 'person' such as gender, birthplace, and education. Attribute data is categorical in nature and can be measured on either a nominal or an ordinal scale [see section 6.2.4].

2 - Quantitative data:
Quantitative data are data that can be counted or measured using measuring equipment like a tape measure, voltmeter or balance. Quantitative data can be divided into discrete and continuous data.

Discrete data can only be discrete values. For example the number of defects or the number of attributes. Measuring data on a discrete scale is like counting. Often, in order to make comparisons of qualitative data we will count the number of measurements falling into each nominal or ordinal category. This creates a quantitative comparison of attribute measurements and is often called discrete or attribute data.

Continuous data are measured on a continuously variable scale, i.e. one that is infinitely divisible, and are sometimes called 'variable data'. Examples of continuous data are: dimensions, time, currency, weight and resistance and are expressed as any real number. Quantitative data is numerical in nature and can be measured on either an interval or a ratio scale [see section 6.2.4]. Sometimes, in order to simplify its reporting or visual representation, we will count the number of continuous data measurements that fall into pre-determined ranges or 'buckets'. This creates discrete or discretized versions of continuous data.

6.2.4 Measurement scales

In order for any measurements to be valid we need to employ well-defined rules of measurement that depend upon the item to be measured. There are four basic measurement scales that should be distinguish between: Nominal, Ordinal, Interval and Ratio.

1 - Nominal scale:

A nominal measurement scale is used to differentiate between items that can be placed in distinct categories but there is no logical and natural order between the categories. The value of an observation belongs in one of the categories and when it is in one category it cannot be in another. For example, measuring 'someone's Blood type: (A+, A-, B+, B-, AB+, AB-, O+)'. There is no order in blood types and a person has just one blood type. Another example of categorical data measured on a nominal scale is 'gender (male or female)'.

2 - Ordinal scale:

An ordinal measurement scale is used to differentiate between items that can be placed in distinct categories and where the categories have an inherent order or relationship. The value of an observation belongs in one of the categories and when it is in one category it cannot be in another, however the differences between the different categories cannot be quantified e.g. measuring 'someone's ranking in a race: (1st, 2nd, 3rd, etc.)'. There is a natural order to the ranking but there is no information about whether it was a close race or whether someone won easily. Another example of categorical data measured on an ordinal scale is 'a company's service level based on a recent transaction (excellent, good, average, poor, very bad)'.

3 - Interval scale:

An interval measurement scale is used to quantify items that have a natural order. The size of differences can be quantified and compared. However, crucially there is an arbitrary zero. In this case it is not possible to say that one interval measurement is some multiple bigger or smaller in size than another interval measurement only that there is a measurable interval between them. This could be for example the 'temperature in an oven: 100°C'. This is hotter than 'temperature in a room: 20°C', but you cannot say the oven is five times hotter than the room. This is because 0°C is actually an arbitrary point on the scale.

4 - Ratio scale:

A ratio measurement scale is used to quantify items that have a natural order. The size of differences can be quantified and compared. Additionally, a meaningful zero exists on a ratio scale which means that it is possible to say that one ratio measurement is a multiple bigger or smaller than another ratio measurement. An example is the height of the Eiffel tower. This can be compared to another building, like the church in your own city center. A height of zero means the ground level of the tower. Another example of a ratio measurement scale would be waiting time at the dentist. Temperature can also be measured on the ratio scale of degrees Kelvin because 0K is defined as absolute zero temperature.

An overview with examples of data types and measurement scales is given in Table 6.2.

Table 6.2. *Data types and Measurement scales*

Data type	Scale type	Natural order	Quantifiable differences	Meaningful zero exists	Example
Qualitative	Nominal	-	-	-	Blood type: (A+, A-, B+, B-, AB+, AB-, O+)
	Ordinal	X	-	-	Performance rating (scale 1 to 5)
Quantitative	Interval	X	X	-	Temp. in an oven is higher than room temperature
	Ratio	X	X	X	Height of tower; number of inhabitants

6

Analyze

6.3 Value Stream Analysis

The objective of 'Value Stream Mapping' (VSM) is to reduce Lead Time and to eliminate Waste. Value Stream Mapping is a technique that is used to analyze the series of activities to manufacture a product or to complete a service. It can be applied to nearly any value chain. Very often it is the first step of each Lean initiative or improvement initiative.

Value Stream Mapping is one the most powerful Lean tools. It links all activities together in one visual representation. As such it provides the bigger picture by illustrating the complete flow and all its connections, which is not only limited to the operational process but also includes material flows, information processes and business processes. Within the visual representation it is possible to distinguish Value Added Activities from Non-Value Added Activities and to identify Waste.

Value Stream Mapping was pioneered in the 1980's by Toyota chief engineer Taiichi Ohno and Sensei (teacher) Shigeo Shingo, with the intention to gain competitive advantage. Value Stream Mapping is a Lean tool and in principle not a quality tool. However, Ohno and Shingo proved that reducing Lead Time and Waste also result in better product quality.

A value stream is defined as the series of all activities required to deliver a product or service. Examples for a Value stream are:

- From raw material to customer delivery.
- From product concept to product launch.
- From customer demand to delivered service.

6.3.1 Value Adding versus Non Value Adding
Like many other quality programs, Lean Six Sigma places the customer in the center of its activities. The first Lean principle is 'Value'. The definition of Value is 'What is of value to the customer'. Even more specific Value means 'The activities the customer is willing to pay for'. It is obvious that by using this definition, not all activities in your process will add value to the customer. So, why do it then? What is the point of doing things nobody wants to pay for?

The purpose of Value Stream Mapping is to visualize the process and distinguish the Value Adding Activities from the Non-Value Adding Activities. Let's review a little more in depth what the meaning of an 'Activity' is. Every activity in your process can be classified as:

1. Value Adding Activities (VA)   Customer is willing to pay for.
2. Non-Value Adding Activities (NVA) Customer is not willing to pay for.
3. Necessary Activities   Necessary for the process.

A Value Adding Activity must meet the following criteria: The customer is willing to pay for the activity; It must be done correctly the first time (First Time Right) and the action must change the product or service in some way. If one of these criteria is not met, the activity is classified as a 'Non-Value Adding Activity' and therefore as 'Waste' or 'Muda', which should be eliminated. Necessary Activities are needed to keep the process running. These activities cannot be taken out of the process easily, but should be limited as much as possible. An example of a Necessary Activity is an inspection required by the customer or by the government.

6.3.2 Value Stream Mapping (Current State)

There is a big difference between Process mapping and Value Stream Mapping, which can, at times, be confusing. Especially in service organizations people might construct a Process map and call it Value stream mapping, but this is not correct. Mapping the process is one of the steps within Value Stream Mapping. In addition flows of material and information are visualized. Also the amount of Work in process, Cycle Times and waiting times are mapped. This is not done in a process map.

It is recommended to construct a so-called 'Door-to-door' Value Stream Map, which examines the bigger picture and accounts for the connections between all processes. For this it is necessary to perform a walk along the whole 'Door-to-door' value stream starting at the end of the value stream and moving upstream. Use a simple paper and pencil to construct the process along the walk. The mapping process is simple, real-time, and iterative, as this method allows for simple corrections.

Figure 58 - *'Brown' paper session*

6

An effective way of working as a group is to cover a wall with paper and provide adhesive notes. Different colors can be used to represent different purposes. Each team member writes their tasks on individual notes and applies them to the paper in sequence. Notes with tasks can easily be moved around as other steps come to mind. The amount of 'Work In Process' (WIP) between each process step is counted. Lines are drawn between the steps to indicate the work flow. Also, lines are drawn to represent the information flows. This is also called a 'Brown paper session', although the paper can be white as well!

The steps to perform Value Stream Mapping are listed below:

1. Define Product Family:
   Group of products with similar process steps that make use of common equipment in the value stream to the customer.
2. Construct Current State Map:
   Identify Waste in the process by mapping the current situation of material flows, work in process and information flows.
3. Construct Future State Map:
   Map the future situation and determine improvements to eliminate Waste.
4. Define Work Plan & Implementation:
   Implement future state map.

VSM Current State - Example

In this section we will construct a Current State Value Stream Map, step by step. This example is based on the fictitious factory 'PEN N.V.' that is assembling pens for its client 'Walmart'.

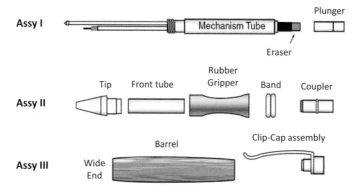

Figure 59 - *Pen assembly overview*

On the opposite page we will visualize the end-result of the Current State Value Stream Map, following the next steps:

- Step 1 – Map customer demand.
- Step 2 – Map production time.
- Step 3 – Map process flow and inventory.
- Step 4 – Add material flow between processes (Push & Pull).
- Step 5 – Add data boxes with current state information.
- Step 6 – Add information flows.
- Step 7 – Add flows for 'Raw components' and 'Finished goods'.
- Step 8 – Add timeline with queue time and Cycle Time.
- Step 9 – Determine Value Added Time.

Although constructing a Value Stream Map is a 'Pencil-and-paper'-tool, we will use a software program called 'Quality Companion' to visualize and analyze the Value Stream Map. This tool is explained in the pen assembly process example, but Value Stream Mapping can also be applied in many other sectors, such as Transactional environments, Logistics and Healthcare.

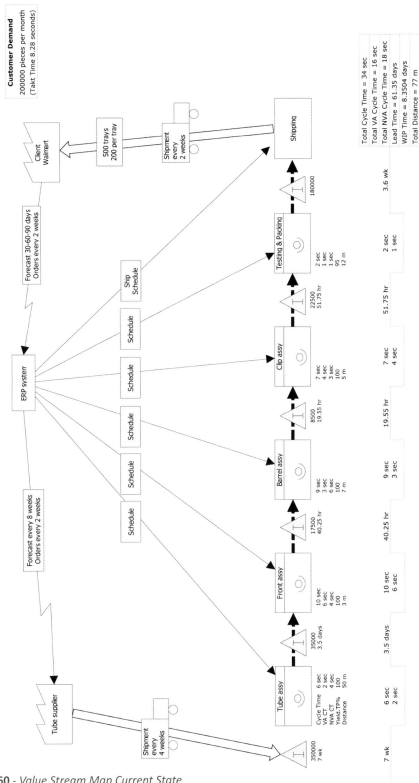

Figure 60 - *Value Stream Map Current State*

Improve

6.4 Reducing Muda (Waste)

Within the Toyota Production System the following three types of variation can be distinguished:

- Muda:
  Waste, uselessness, non-value added or idleness.
- Muri:
  Overburden, impossible, beyond one's power or excessiveness.
- Mura:
  Unevenness, irregularity or lack of uniformity.

These are also called the 3 Ms of Lean. The reduction of these three types of Waste is fundamental within the Toyota Production System to increase effectiveness and profitability. For each of the three types we will review a number of principles and techniques to reduce the types of variation.

6.4.1 Waste identification (for the Operation)

Reducing Muda can be achieved by assuring that a process will not consume more resources than are necessary to produce the goods or provide the service that the customer actually wants. Reducing Muda can be achieved by avoiding activities that do not add value to the product, meaning producing 'First Time Right', without loss of materials, loss of resources, rework, repair and waiting. In most Lean programs this is the first variation that will be addressed, because it is easier distinguished than the other types. Also redesigning processes or products (Innovation) can result in using less resources.

A Value Adding Activity must meet the following criteria: The customer is willing to pay for the activity; It must be done correctly the first time and the action must change the product or service in some way. If one of these criteria is not met, the activity is classified as a 'Non-Value Adding Activity' and therefore as 'Waste' or 'Muda', which should be eliminated. Initially there were 7 types of Waste, but many acknowledge also an 8th type of Waste.

	1.	**Over-production**	Producing more than asked by market
	2.	**Waiting**	Goods or documents not being processed
	3.	**Transport**	Transporting materials or products
	4.	**Over-processing**	Taking unneeded steps to process parts
	5.	**Inventory**	Unnecessary supplies or stock
	6.	**Movement**	Searching and unnecessary movements
	7.	**Defects**	Faults, scrap or bad quality
	8.	**Unused expertise**	Not using existing expertise or knowledge

Figure 61 - *Muda: 8 types of Waste*

1 - Overproduction:
Overproduction occurs when more products are produced than are required at a certain time by the internal or external customer. One common practice that leads to this Muda is the production of large batches.

Overproduction is considered the worst Muda because it hides and/or generates all the others. Overproduction leads to excess inventory, which then requires the expenditure of resources on storage space and preservation, activities that do not benefit the customer. There is also the possibility that customer demand or customer requirements change. As a consequence goods might become obsolete or services will be provided while there is no customer request (anymore).

2 - Waiting:
Whenever goods or documents are not being processed, these are waiting. Waiting is not about people who are waiting, but goods or documents that are waiting to be processed. In traditional processes this is mostly the largest type of Waste. Waiting for information or approval in order to continue the process is also classified as 'Waiting'.

3 - Transportation:
Each time a product is moved between process steps we qualify it as Waste. Transportation between operation steps does not make any transformation to the product that the consumer is willing to pay for. Transport therefore adds to costs without adding value. There is also a risk of the product or service being damaged, lost, delayed, etc.

4 - Over-processing:
Over-processing occurs any time work is done to the product for which the customer is not willing to pay. Examples are the use of components that are more precise, complex, expensive, or higher quality than absolutely required. In service organizations it means unnecessary inspections, verifications and stamps. It also means unnecessary, redundant or superfluous information.

6

Measuring quality or inspection is also classified as 'Over-processing' as long as the measurement is used for verification only and not used to adjust or improve the quality of the product. Unfortunately many companies cannot do without inspection in order to deliver good products or services. This is due to a low performance capability and low reliability of the process.

5 - Inventory:
Inventory is the excessive quantity of raw materials or excessive semi-finished products (Work-in-Process) between operations and finished goods. Inventory represents a capital outlay that has not yet produced an income either by the producer or for the consumer. In service organizations inventory refers to documents (complaints, requests, orders etc.) waiting between operations in the process.

A certain amount of inventory is needed in order to assure 'Flow' in the process, but it should be limited as much as possible. In a situation where activities within the process are perfectly balanced, there is almost no inventory between operations. Slowly reducing the amount of inventory is the best way to realize the opportunities for improvement.

6 - Motion:
Motion refers to the movement (walking) of operators and employees from one activity to the other activity. Searching for information (not walking) is also classified as 'Motion', because during the searching process no value is added to the product.

7 - Defects:
Products with defects cannot be delivered to the consumer. Documents that are not complete and perfectly clear to the customer are also classified as 'Defects'. Not producing 'First Time Right' (FTR) is classified as 'Defects' as well.
In the event the product can be repaired or reworked, it requires resources to do so. If it cannot be repaired or reworked, it should be scrapped. In both cases extra costs are incurred for reworking, new components, rescheduling etc.

8 - Unused expertise:
Initially there were only 7 types of Waste. The 8th type of Waste has been added later. Not using the available knowledge, skills or expertise that is present in the organization, is also Waste. Young people can learn from older people. Management can learn from the expertise at the shop floor etc.

6.4.2 Waste identification (for the Customer)
One redefinition of 'Operational Waste', that better fit service operations, is called 'Customer Service Waste', (Bicheno and Holweg, 2009). They defined the following list of Wastes that is often used in Lean Service programs to improve the customer journey:

1 - Opportunity Loss:
An opportunity lost to retain or win customers, a failure to establish rapport, ignoring customers, unfriendliness, and rudeness.

2 - Delay:
Delay on the part of customers waiting for service, for delivery, in queues, for response, not arriving as promised. The customer's time may seem free to the provider, but when she takes custom elsewhere the pain begins.

3 - Unnecessary Movement:
Queuing several times, lack of one-stop, poor ergonomics in the service encounter.

4 - Duplication:
Having to re-enter data, repeat details on forms, copy information across, answer queries from several sources within the same organization.

5 - Incorrect inventory:
Being out-of-stock, unable to get exactly what was required, substitute products or services.

6 - Unclear Communication:
Unclear communication, and the wastes of seeking clarification, confusion over product or service use, wasting time finding a location that may result in misuse or duplication.

7 - Errors:
Errors in the service transaction, product or service defects in the product-service bundle, lost or damaged goods, lack of quality in service processes.

6.5 Reducing Muri (Overburden)

Reducing Muri can be achieved by producing according Takt Time and implementing 'Flow' and Standardized Work. Flow should be observable and every process step must be reduced to its simplest elements or components. The number of different components and specialized steps throughout the organization should be limited. Limiting the number of different screws for instance will result in less tools, less training, less stock, less mistakes etc. A World Class example of this is the truck producer Scania. This principle is also known as 'Smart customization'. Muri can also be avoided by not pushing equipment or employees to the edge of what they are capable of. Working overtime for a longer period, bad ergonomics and postponing preventive maintenance will increase the risk of Muri.

6.5.1 Flow

One of the Lean principles is 'Flow'. Taking a walk on the shop floor with an experienced Belt or Lean Sensei, the first question to be answered is 'Where is the Flow'? Flow should be visible at the shop floor. This should not be compared with people being busy. Everybody can look very busy, without having a Flow. Lean is focused on getting the right things to the right place at the right time in the right quantity to achieve perfect Flow. If operation flows perfectly without interruptions there is no inventory or only a limited amount of inventory between process steps. This results in a lower risk off confusion and mistakes. Flow will create a continuous process to identify problems. Each problem becomes an opportunity for improvement.

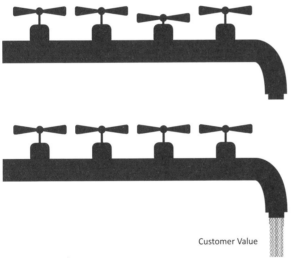

Customer Value

Figure 62 - *Flow*

6

If you experience no Flow, there is no Lean. The easiest way to observe flow is to take a look at both 'doors' of the shop floor. At one door you should see orders coming in (e.g. parts, components, sick patients, clients, bins, trucks, requests, etc.). At the other door you see finished goods and completed products going out (e.g. subassemblies, healthy patients, happy clients, products, passports, answers, etc.) going out. Between these two 'Doors' you should see people busy and equipment running, but more important is that you observe Flow at each work location or machine. At one side of the work location you should see work being done and on the other side of the location you should see work that is completed and moved to the next operation step. The amount of work waiting should be limited, organized and clear.

A steady and continuous Flow can be observed easily because the time for work to move between stations is constant. The amount of time depends on the type of organization, but will typically vary between a few seconds and a few minutes. It should not take hours, days or even longer. Even for very complex processes it should be possible to observe Flow. A good example is the production of trucks or treating a patient in a hospital.

Sometimes it is not possible to move the product between stations. Examples are building a house or a ship. This is very often experienced in 'Engineering-to-Order' (ETO) organizations where each product is designed and build to customer specification. When it is not possible to move the product, then Flow can be experienced by bringing pieces of work to the location. It is possible to apply the Flow principle in the preparation of work packages and in the scheduling process of the people working at the product. When you see the product standing alone, without a person working on it there is no Flow. No value is added to the product when no person is making a change to the product, even if other people have done preparatory work. If you see a group of people standing around the equipment, discussing what to do but not performing changes to the product there is no Flow.

Lean organizations always take the product as the base. As soon as the first added value activity on a certain product starts, it should be moved through the process in such a way that the total Lead Time is limited as much as possible. The equipment, the people or the departments are not leading, but the product should be leading. You can compare this with a trauma patient arriving in the hospital. Every part of the organization is focused on getting the patient through the process as quick as possible.

It is important that the Cycle Time of the process will match the Takt Time of the customer as much as possible. If the Cycle Time of the slowest operation step is longer than the Takt Time, it will not be possible to deliver the product or service on time. If the Cycle Time of the slowest operation step is less than the Takt Time, there is a risk of overproduction.

Ideally the Cycle Time should be equal to the Takt Time. However, the reality is that demand is dynamic and process disruptions can occur (e.g. unplanned downtime, employee sickness etc.). Therefore it is recommended to organize the Cycle Time in such way that the time of the operation steps will be slightly less than the Takt Time of the customer. It is even better to make the cycle time flexible by enabling variation of workload in the production cells by simply varying the number of employees/machines.

In the VSM example the Takt Time can be calculated as follows:

$$Takt\ Time = \frac{Available\ Work\ Time}{Customer\ Demand} = \frac{3\times(8-\frac{1}{3})\times20\times3,600}{(200,000)} = 8.28\ sec\ per\ part$$

Conclusion: the optimal speed of the slowest process should be producing a part every 8.28 seconds.

6.5.2 Work balancing

In processes, often one employee or machine has a high workload while at the same time other employees or machines are underutilized. The workload between the activities should be balanced as much as possible to avoid unevenness in the process.

Let's review the process of handling requests for getting an internet connection. Time studies are performed for the four employees involved in the process. This shows that the average Cycle Time of the first stage (A) appears to be 6 minutes. The following three process steps take respectively 10, 3 and 4 minutes. The speed of the entire process follows the speed of the slowest process step, which is a Cycle time of 10 minutes. The process cannot deliver any faster than one request each 10 minutes.

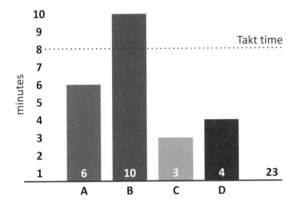

Figure 63 - *Before work balancing*

It appears that the actual Takt time is 8 minutes, meaning the process is not fast enough to handle customer requests in time. The team is asked to redesign the process in such a way that it is able to meet this Takt time. Together they evaluate whether activities can be arranged in a different way between the operation steps. It appears that activities from the slowest process step B can be moved to process steps C and D, as is represented in Figure 64.

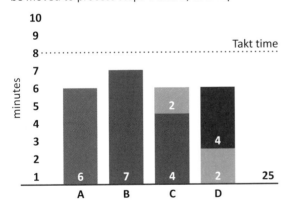

Figure 64 - *After work balancing*

Although the sum of activities now takes 25 minutes instead of 23 minutes, the process is now able to handle customer requests within a Cycle time of 7 minutes which is faster than the Takt time of 8 minutes.

6.5.3 Total Productive Maintenance (TPM)

'Total Productive Maintenance' (TPM) focuses on the effective and efficient use of equipment, by avoiding breakdowns, delays and machine-related rejections. This is achieved by methods used to ensure that more is produced using existing machinery. TPM is mainly used in production environments that are highly machine dependent such as automotive, food and processing industry. As a method it is rarely applied in office environments, although reliable hardware and software are of course very important for office employees.

Preventive maintenance was developed by U.S. factories that supply the military during the second world war. After the war preventive maintenance was introduced in Japan (1951). Nippon Denso (Toyota Group) was the first company to introduce preventive maintenance plant wide (1960). Nippon-Denso was awarded the distinguished plant prize for developing and implementing TPM, by the Japanese Institute of Plant Maintenance (JIPM). Therefore, Nippon-Denso became the first company to obtain the TPM certification. In 1987 the first real TPM initiative in the U.S. was developed by the Kodak's Tennessee Eastman facility.

Nowadays maintenance cost are a major issue for many organizations, but instead of just looking at actual costs, most organizations look at the Total life cycle costs of a piece of equipment. Investment in a plant occurs from its early development. The return of the investment therefore should also begin soon after its commissioning. It should be the objective of every company to maximize the life-time profitability of its equipment. To realize this objective, the eight pillars of TPM play an important role.

The TPM approach is visualized in a House with eight pillars, as demonstrated in Figure 65. We will briefly review each of the pillars. It is not the intention to review the implementation of TPM in detail, but to address the importance of reliable equipment in achieving stable and effective processes. As such, it is very important in Lean Six Sigma initiatives. The first two pillars are very effective in the first two maturity levels. Specifically the pillar 'Autonomous Maintenance' involves operators in 5S and problem solving initiatives. This will contribute to the creation of an improvement culture based on ownership and it will improve equipment reliability.

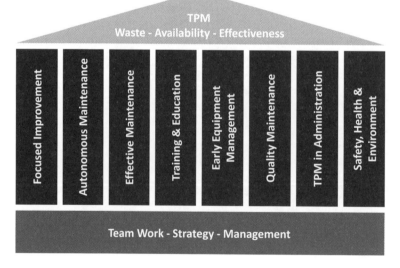

Figure 65 - *TPM House of Quality*

At the Yellow and Orange Belt it is important they understand the meaning of Focused Improvement and Autonomous Maintenance. We will therefore explain these first two pillars only.

1 - Focused Improvement:
Focused Improvement (also called Kobetsu Kaizen), is a process of Continuous Improvement activities with Zero Wastes, Zero Breakdowns, Zero Defects and Zero Accidents as objectives. The Focused Improvement process is driven by the Overall Equipment Effectiveness (OEE) performance measure.

2 - Autonomous Maintenance:
Autonomous Maintenance (also called Jishu Hozen), deals with making operators responsible for their piece of equipment and tooling, rather than having maintenance done by special maintenance technicians. Giving operators the responsibility for good equipment condition, cleanliness and lubrication helps to achieve a high level of ownership amongst operating teams. This pillar is a necessary requirement for Zero breakdowns, and has an indirect effect in achieving Zero Waste, Zero Defects and Zero Accidents.

6

6.5.4 Competence Management

The leveling of workload between operations will reduce unevenness and Muri. However, in some cases the inefficient distribution of competencies of employees across the different operation steps is a roadblock for workload leveling. For some operation steps you may have an adequate number of people who can perform the operation step, while simultaneously you may have a limited number of people who have the skills for performing another operation step. This will limit the flexibility of the organization to move people around operations if needed. Try to identify which competencies are a roadblock for work leveling and which activities can only be executed by one person. What will happen if this person is on holiday, gets sick or will find a different job?

Revision Date:		7/5/2014
Symbol	Level	
⊕	Can not perform task	
⊕	Familiar with elements of the job	
◑	Can perform with help	
◕	Can perform solo	
●	Can teach others to perform	

Accounting											
Process / Name	Bill Entry	Bill Pay	Invoicing	Receiving Payments	Credit Card Transactions	Reconciliations	Customer Account Entry	Expense Report Review	Expense Report Entry	Creating POs	Banking Deposits
Marcie	●	●	●	●	●	●	●	●	●	●	●
Michell	◕	◕	●	◕	◑	⊕	●	◕	⊕	◕	●
	⊕	⊕	⊕	⊕	⊕	⊕	⊕	⊕	⊕	⊕	⊕

Figure 66 - *Competence matrix*

At the same time many organizations make no distinction in the level of expertise that employees need to execute an operation. In the Figure 66 we can distinguish five different levels of expertise from 'Cannot perform task' to 'Can teach others to perform'.

This approach will give the department manager or team leader a tool to define what competencies should be developed and what competencies are available sufficiently within the department. It can also help clarify the need to train employees. It also gives clarity in the difference between a very experienced employee and a less experienced employee. A program to increase the competencies in a structured way, will improve the flexibility of a department. Combining this with standardization across the different departments will also increase the flexibility of the entire organization, because it will be easier to shift an employee from one department to another. It will also avoid Muri, by assigning employees on tasks that they are not capable of.

6.6 Reducing Mura (Unevenness)

A common misunderstanding is that improving productivity is working faster. Lean however has not the intention to treat every job as a sprint and to complete every task as soon as possible. Lean is not about increasing speed, but about reducing unevenness in speed in order to increase predictability which will create a smooth and regular basis for further improvement initiatives.

"The slower but consistent tortoise causes less waste and is much more desirable
than the speedy hare that races ahead and then stops occasionally to doze.
The Toyota Production System can be realized only when all workers become tortoise."
Taiichi Ohno

Unevenness in production is called Mura. Reducing Mura can be achieved by production leveling, by product leveling and through following the 'Just In Time' principle. Reducing Mura will result in a minimum of inventory on the shop floor. In order to avoid shortages and late deliveries of parts it is necessary to develop a forecasting system to predict demand for process steps and suppliers for long Lead Times or changeover time.

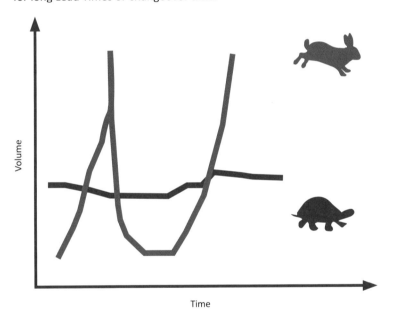

Figure 67 - *Rather 'Slow but steady'*

6.6.1 Pull

Imagine what would happen if every operation in the process produced the amount of parts that it is capable of without alignment of the amounts needed by the other processes. This will result in a chaos with huge piles of parts around the respective machines. These piles are pushed to the next process step in the operation in order to create space. Increasing the efficiency of only a single machine or process step will increase the logistical chaos even more. It will result in excessive quantities of raw materials and excessive semi-finished products. Observing many different products on the shop floor, and many people being very busy is a signal that the organization is not Lean. As mentioned earlier: excessive Inventory means Waste. Lean organizations are organized, have oversight and demonstrate no stress.

Nevertheless, many operations apply Push. Sometimes even without realizing it. Operation managers are focusing on optimizing individual process steps or equipment especially when it concerns expensive equipment. Also a backlog in the delivery process will result in Push-behavior, when managers and logistical planners are pushing new orders into the operational process. Push can result in overproduction of finished products waiting for a customer that might never come. Overproduction is called the worst type of Waste, because all resources have been used and you cannot be sure if the product will be sold.

To avoid Waste, it is necessary to work according the 'Just In Time' (JIT) principle. This can be achieved by supplying each operation step in the process with the right part, at the right time, in the right amount. This can be achieved by implementing Pull, which is the fourth Lean principle. Working according Pull instead of Push will avoid inventory and overproduction (which is explained in Figure 68 and Figure 69). This starts with the demand of the customer, who pulls first! Pull means that the subsequent process determines the number of items that needs to be delivered by the downstream process.

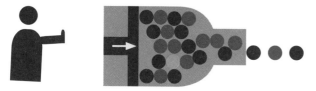

Figure 68 - *Push:*
Output: 1 part per minute
Inventory: 24 parts

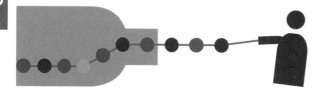

Figure 69 - *Pull:*
Output: 1 part per minute
Inventory: 10 parts

Pull can be applied in the process before the so-called 'De-coupling point'. This is the point where products will turn from generic parts to customer specific parts. The de-coupling point is the point where the forecast-driven elements (Pull) meet the demand-driven elements (Push). An inventory buffer will always be needed just before the de-coupling point to cater for the discrepancy between the sales forecast and the actual demand (i.e. the forecast error).

Pull can be achieved by the use of tools like Kanban and One-Piece-Flow, which will be explained in the next sections.

Kanban

Kanban is one of the tools through which 'Just In Time' and Pull are achieved. It was developed at Toyota by Taiichi Ohno. Kanban systems control the logistical chain between operation steps, by aligning inventory levels with actual consumption. It is not an inventory control system though. Kanban systems allow each sub-process to withdraw from the downstream sub-processes only the parts needed in the amount that is needed. The Kanban itself is a physical card or a digital signal which is sent to the preceding process step to indicate that certain parts are needed. Such a Kanban is called a withdrawal Kanban. It contains information about the parts that are needed, like the amount and specification. The earlier process delivers exactly the number of items that are indicated by the Kanban. The process will not produce parts when there is no production Kanban (no demand).

A Kanban is sometimes called a 'Supermarket', as the development of Kanban is based on the way supermarkets schedule demand. In a supermarket customers obtain the required quantity at the required time, no more and no less. The supermarket puts only products on the shelves that are expected to be sold within a certain timeframe. Customers take only what they need for the next couple of days, no more. Lean organizations should treat each process step both as an internal client to upstream processes and as an internal supplier for downstream processes. As a client it should request no more than is needed for the timeframe and as a supplier it should prepare or produce no more than what is requested by its customer.

Figure 70 - *Warehouse Kanban card*

6

Two-bin system

A Two-bin system is a special Kanban system that is often applied for standard parts and small items. At a certain work location a rack is placed with a number of positions. Each position can contain two boxes (bins) for a certain item. When the box is empty, it will be placed behind the filled box or at the bottom of the rack as is shown in Figure 71. There is no Kanban card since the empty box itself is the Kanban. In some cases there might be a flag available at the back of the rack that indicates that an empty box needs to be replaced by a full one. When the box contains standard (inexpensive) parts like screws or bolts, the amount in the box is not counted but is weighted or just filled. For inexpensive articles a two-bin system is cheaper than controlling the stock by an ERP (Enterprise Resource Planning) system.

Figure 71 - *Two bin system*

6

In office environments this system can be used in many situations for small items like pens, paper or other office supplies. The empty box is delivered to the departments secretary who will order new pens. The system is also applied a lot in hospitals for small items like bandages or needles.

Figure 72 - *Kanban in Hospital*

FIFO lane

Applying Type leveling and One-Piece Flow in production can be achieved by applying FIFO lanes that can hold only a certain amount of parts or products. FIFO stands for 'First-In-First-Out'. The purpose of this system is to reduce and control inventory between process steps. It is the responsibility of the planning department to place customer orders in the right sequence according to demand and certain priority rules. It is the responsibility of the operation department to complete the requested orders in the right sequence, without changing priorities again.

While Kanban systems are applied before the de-coupling point, FIFO lanes can be applied after the de-coupling point, at the location in the process where products become customer specific or model specific. Let's consider a mass producer of four different types of headphones. The company receives customer orders from their clients for one of the models; A, B, C or D. The de-coupling point in the process is the point where it is determined if a headphone will be model A, B, C or D. The planning department sends the order to the de-coupling point of the production line. After this point orders will follow the First-In-First-Out concept until the headphones are completed. Also, there should be minimum inventory levels from the de-coupling point to the end of the line.

A FIFO lane can be a belt or trolley that is used to move products between stations. The products will remain in the same order and cannot overtake each other. If the FIFO lane is full, no Kanban is released to the upstream process until inventory is used up. In some cases employees can sit next to each other and can move the parts to each other. One-Piece Flow is the most optimum way of moving parts.

Scheduling the Pacemaker

In a Lean organization the scheduling instructions are introduced only at one point in the 'Door-to-door value stream'. Controlling the so-called pacemaker process sets the pace for all downstream processes. Upstream the pacemaker process we have to apply Pull, using supermarkets and Kanban cards. At the same time FIFO lanes will be applied after the pacemaker to assure Flow.

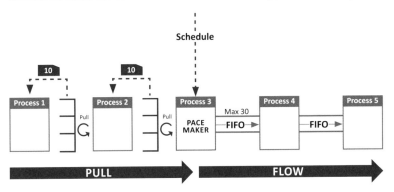

Figure 73 - *Scheduling the Pacemaker*

6.6.2 Volume and Type leveling

Mura relates to variations in production. These are on the one hand caused by variations in the requested volume, and on the other hand by a variation in type. An organization should focus on reducing variation and also to cope with variations better. This will lead to a more flexible production with less stress and fewer errors. In Japanese this principle to reduce unevenness is called Heijunka, which means production leveling or production smoothing. In this section we will discuss two elements volume leveling and type leveling.

Volume Leveling

Volume leveling means that organizations will operated at levels of long-term average demand. Inventory buffers need to be kept proportional to the variability in demand, stability of production process and shipping speed. Heijunka also indicates if production is ahead of schedule or behind schedule.

Organizations can apply certain tools and scheduling rules to ensure that the process has as little encumbrance as possible due to fluctuations in customer demand. Most organizations will have little influence on fluctuations in customer demand though. You simply cannot tell the customer when to order a product or service. One way to cope with this fact is to try to improve the predictability of demand. Most organizations will have some kind of prediction model and sales forecasts, which will help them to anticipate on fluctuations in demand. For some organizations it is easier to develop such models than for others as all business are different. Some organizations have seasonal demands, some have an extensive variety of different products, while others have a very regular and stable demand of one single product. However, it appears that even the emergency department of a hospital is able to predict the amount of patients that will arrive at certain days of the week and at certain times, by analyzing historical data. A good prediction of demand can be used to define the number of resources that will be needed. Techniques that support production leveling are Heijunka boxes, Kanban and CONWIP scheduling.

In Figure 74 you will find order schedules for two departments A and B. Both schedules have a loading of 280 products in a week. Department A demonstrates an enormous fluctuation in loading, as it is not leveled. Department B demonstrates a loading of 40 pieces every day. Once every month a forecast is made to verify if a loading of '40 pieces per day' is still in line with the Takt Time of the clients.

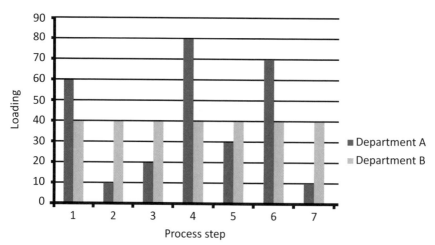

Figure 74 - *Work leveling (department B)*

Type leveling

The essence of Type leveling is to make every part every day. Type leveling in a transactional environment involves for instance scheduling meetings at a fixed time of the day, week or month. Another example is to categorize performance measures in groups that will be reviewed each day, each week or each month. As such type leveling improves predictability. Everybody knows what to do and when.

Let's consider the mass production of kids bikes. The manufacturer receives orders from department stores for one of the models; A, B or C. Since the company is trying to minimize waste around equipment changeovers, the production schedule as represented in Figure 75 (left): 15 times model A, 10 times model B and 5 times model C.

However, it might happen that last minute a client decides that volumes of model A need to be model B instead and that volumes for model C suddenly increase. These kinds of changes put an enormous amount of pressure on the manufacturer. For example, imagine that a large batch of model C is already in production, causing an increased Lead Time for model A, that is produced on the same production line. The planning department might now choose to stop the order that is already in production. Another option might be to increase resources, capacity and inventory when the change in demand is encountered. The customer services department will have to work overtime to discuss the resultant late deliveries with clients and redefine priorities together with sales and planning. This example might look exaggerated, but it is pretty common in many organizations. Running your organization as a mass producer will increase Waste. To avoid such waste the principle of 'Type leveling' should be applied. This is represented in the right part of Figure 75.

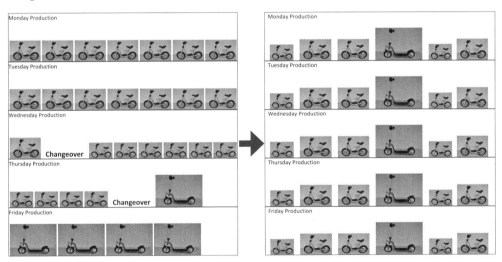

Figure 75 - *Type leveling (before and after)*

One-Piece Flow
A term that is related to Type leveling is 'One-Piece Flow', which demonstrates that the ultimate goal of an organization should be to be able to produce one single product at any moment. It might sound strange, but One-Piece Flow does not necessarily mean 'One-Piece', but can also refer to a very small batch size.

An advantage of One-Piece Flow is that quality problems will be discovered earlier. Imagine that bike model A has a problem with the brakes. In the traditional situation we would have produced 15 bikes of model A before the mistake was discovered at the downstream process. In the new situation we would have produced only one bike of model A when the problem was discovered. Since the operation is now more flexible we will be able to postpone the production of model A for a while so that the problem can be solved. Once that is done, the production of model A can be resumed.

Batch production:

- Every process step has its own inventory.
- Production is moved in batches.

Figure 76 - *Batch production*

One-Piece Flow:

- No inventory between process steps.
- Production is moved by single piece.

Figure 77 - *One-Piece Flow*

Service organizations should try to reduce batches and aim for One-Piece Flow as well. Although you might feel that working in batches is more effective, it is not. The best way to convince people is to show them a few movies that can easily be found on YouTube. This will explain the concept far better than a verbal explanation would. Challenges that service organizations experience in changing-over are very often related to limitations in IT-systems and limitations in employees competencies. The limitations in the IT-system are related to logging in and out to different systems and systems not being integrated. Improving transactional processes is therefore very often related to improvements in IT-systems.

Implementing Type leveling or One Piece Flow will increase the amount of changeovers. This seems illogical but the reduction of Waste, the need for less capacity and an increased flexibility is in favor of Type leveling/One-Piece Flow. It does emphasize the need for efficient changeover times and smart inventory buffers. Type leveling therefore cannot be implemented without Quick Changeover initiatives. This can be achieved by Skill development of employees, by improving IT-systems in transactional processes or by SMED projects. The SMED technique will be reviewed in the next section.

Lowering the water level

As mentioned earlier 'Seeking Perfection' is one of the Lean principles. A way to drive Continuous Improvement is 'Lowering the water level'. This is a metaphor of a boat on a river and a number of rocks at the bottom of the river. If a company is not Lean, problems are hidden in a 'sea of resources'.

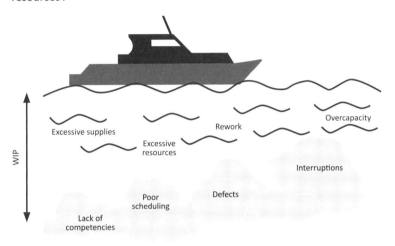

Figure 78 - *When an organization is not Lean*

This water level is equivalent to the amount of resources, labor, equipment and intermediate goods. It is also equivalent to the amount of orders and work in progress on the shop floor. The higher the water level, the more resources and work in progress is present on the shop floor. If an organization has many hidden problems, there are many rocks at the bottom of the river. The organization also needs a lot of water to make sure that the process does not get stuck.

For someone who has no experience with Lean it may seem like it goes well with this organization. Everyone is very busy, all equipment runs and there are many orders. But a 'high water level' is an indication that there are hidden problems in the organization. If an employee experiences a problem, he will place one order aside and continues with the next order. As a result orders will end up in a queue for processing, inspection or transport. As mentioned earlier these are all examples of Waste (Muda). We have previously explained that the average processing time will increase when increasing the level of work in progress (Little's Law). Therefore, a high water level is equal to long lead times. Further, if a problem is not solved, there is a risk that the same problem will occur again.

Lean states that problems should be fixed before continuing the operation. Highlighting the problem areas and identifying the 'rocks' that we need to eliminate first, can be done by lowering the water level. Lowering the amount of WIP on the shop floor can be done by reducing the number of orders in the system. Problems will be exposed by 'lowering the water level'. By eliminating problems (rocks) we become Lean.

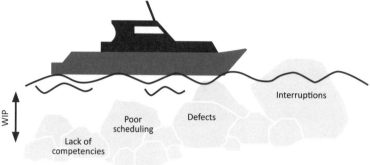

Figure 79 - *When an organization starts to be Lean*

Be careful not to lower the water level too fast. An operation might come to an abrupt end when it hits too many rocks at the same time. The ultimate risk is that the operation will stop completely and will not be able to deliver any orders anymore. This is of course not the intention of implementing Lean. The purpose of seeking perfection is to improve continuously, taking small steps. When hitting one rock, you should increase the water level a little bit, making sure production can continue. Then you should start a Kaizen initiative to remove the rock. Then you can continue lowering the water level again. So the process of removing the obstacles should be steady, one step at a time.

6

6.6.3 Quick Change Over (SMED)

The aim for One-Piece Flow or smaller batch sizes can cause logistical problems at complex equipment, because it requires a changeover. Changing a mold for instance requires a lot of time and changing-over after every single product does not make sense. According to Shigeo Shingo a winning team cannot survive without quick change-overs. Undoubtedly, the best example for this is demonstrated by changing the tires in the pit stop during a formula 1 race. The world record for changing all four tires is around 2 seconds! This requires a smart design, proper preparation, training and excellent teamwork.

cjmac / Shutterstock.com

Figure 80 - *The winning team*

To translate the F1 pit stop approach to the manufacturing process, Shigeo Shingo develop the SMED-process at Mazda, Mitsubishi and Toyota from 1950 to 1960. Shingo called the initiative to reduce the changeover time 'SMED - Single Minute Exchange of Dies', where single minute refers to 'one digit', meaning less than 10 minutes'. SMED is an analytical method with the objective to reduce materials, skilled resources and time necessary to set-up equipment. This also includes the time that is needed to run smoothly after a changeover. The advantages of quick changeovers include increased availability, greater flexibility, shorter Lead Times, less start-up losses and prevention of investments.

The SMED approach incorporates an eight step approach:

1. Choose project.
2. Evaluate current achievements.
3. Define internal & external activities.
4. Categorize internal activities externally.
5. Streamline the process (eliminate adjustment activities).
6. Test proposed changes.
7. Verify results.
8. Implement improvements.

An important element to reduce the changeover time is to move activities as much as possible outside the time of the actual changeover (when the production process is stopped). External activities like preparation and cleaning can be done while the machine is still running.

6.7 Value Stream Improvement

It is not the intention of drawing a Current State VSM to identify Waste, problems and improvement opportunities and to immediately solve each one. This is not efficient, and will most likely not help achieve the real potential benefits. The purpose of the Current State VSM is to provide the basis for designing the Future State VSM.

6.7.1 Value Stream Mapping (Future State)

Designing the optimal Value Stream is done behind a desk. The outcome is called the 'Future State Value Stream Map'. You will find that the end result will be totally different than whatever you have imagined on the Gemba or by making some quick-wins. The resultant Future State map will be the optimal logistical flow that can be used for the next 1-3 years.

Questions that will be answered during constructing the Future State map are:

- What sources of waste can be identified?
- Where can we implement continuous flow?
- Where do we need pull systems (Kanban) to manage upstream production processes?
- What is the pacemaker or bottle neck in our process?
- How do we level the workload?
- How can we prevent failures and deliver 'First Time Right'?

In the previous sections we reviewed several tools and techniques to reduce Muda, Mura and Muri. These tools can be used to construct the Future State Value Stream Map. Not all tools have to be used in each situation. Which tools should be used depends on the situation. In Figure 81 an example is shown of the Future state Value Stream Map. We will not explain all the details of this figure, because this tool is composed by Green and Black Belts.

6

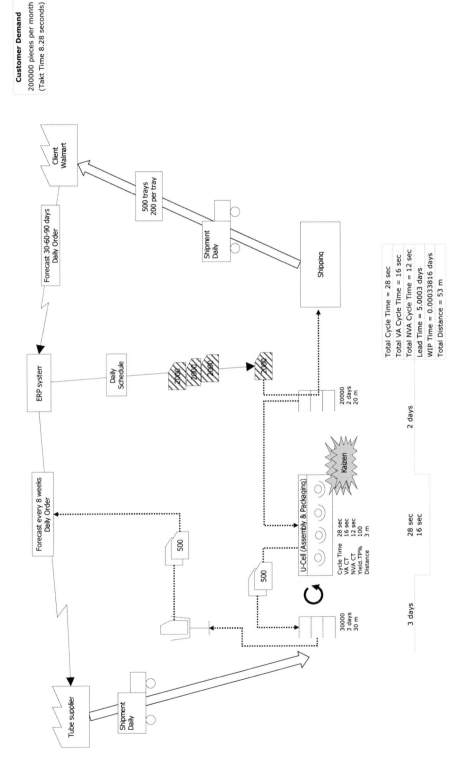

Figure 81 - *Value Stream Map - Future State*

6

Control

6.8 First Time Right

Making an error is human. You can expect dedication and commitment from employees, but you cannot expect that employees will never make mistakes. Below a number of human mistakes is listed:

- Forgetfulness.
- Misunderstanding.
- Incorrect identification.
- Lack of experience.
- Arrogance or being (too) fastidious about rules or details.
- Inadvertency or sloppiness.
- Slowness.
- Not following the standard.
- Surprise (unexpected machine operation, etc.).
- Intentional (sabotage).

You also have to keep in mind so-called 'Red Flag Conditions', meaning that the probability that errors will happen is high in certain situations. Consider the following conditions and realize what might happen:

- Lack of Standardized Work (everyone needs to be a specialist).
- Symmetry (a component can be mounted in different ways).
- Rapid repetition (too fast to handle).
- High volume (too much to handle adequately).
- Poor environmental conditions (high temperature, bad lighting making a task more difficult).
- Adjustments (changes in forms, equipment, design, process etc.).
- Start-up new series (changes in documents, tooling etc.).
- Many or mixed parts (confusing overview).
- Multiple steps for one person (confusing the ability to see progress at a glance).
- Non-frequent production (no experience, no rhythm).

It is the employee's responsibility to be dedicated, but it is the system's responsibility to prevent mistakes. In order to reduce the Cost of Poor Quality, it is necessary to produce 'First Time Right' (FTR) by preventing mistakes and damage, rather than repairing or inspecting. In the control phase we focus on delivering the right products, fit for purpose and without quality problems. The best way to address this is during the design phase of the product or service and to design a feature or constraint to prevent the mistake. We will discuss this in the section about Poka Yoke. We will also review how to perform a process risk analysis (pFMEA) for a Control plan.

Figure 82 - *First Time Right*

6.8.1 Process FMEA (PFMEA)

'Process Failure Mode and Effect Analysis' (PFMEA) is a structured risk analysis method that is used to identify potential failure modes in processes, products or services and to plan actions so that the negative effects will be minimized. It was one of the first systematic techniques of failure analysis. The FMEA is sometimes called PFMEA, meaning process-FMEA.

Figure 83 - *Cause & Effect*

FMEA was developed in the 1950s to study problems that might arise from malfunctions of military systems. In 1993 the Automotive Industry Action Group (AIAG) and the American Society of Quality Control (ASQC) established the standardized FMEA method as a part of APQP. Ford, GM and Chrysler describe FMEA steps in an FMEA manual. Today, FMEA is used more and more in industry, high-tech and other sectors like service providers. FMEA includes review of the following:

- The process (the activities)
- Failure modes (what could go wrong?)
- Failure causes (why would the failure happen?)
- Failure effects (what would be the consequences of each failure?)

Teams apply FMEA analysis to evaluate processes for possible failures and to prevent them by correcting the processes proactively, rather than reacting to adverse events after failures have occurred. FMEA is particularly useful in evaluating a new process prior to implementation and in assessing the impact of a proposed change to an existing process.

A FMEA identifies the opportunities of failure (failure modes), in each step of the process. Each failure mode gets a numeric score that reflects the likelihood that the failure will occur, the likelihood that the failure will not be detected and the amount of harm the failure mode may cause to a person or the damage the failure mode may cause to a system or equipment.

12 Steps to construct a PFMEA:

1.	Process Step/Item	Record process steps or component of a product.
2.	Function	Functions of process step or product component/system
3.	Requirements	Requirements necessary to perform the functions
4.	Potential Failure Mode	Potential failure if requirement isn't met.
5.	Effect	What is the effect of the potential failure?
6.	Severity	The severity of the effect to the customer or production process.
7.	Cause	Determine cause of the failure (Ishikawa, 5x Why).
8.	Current Controls	Current prevention/ detection of measures.
9.	Occurrence	Estimate the chance of failure occurrence.
10.	Detection	How well can failures/causes be detected?
11.	Risk Priority Number	RPN = Severity × Occurrence × Detection.
12.	Improvement Actions	How can product/process be improved?

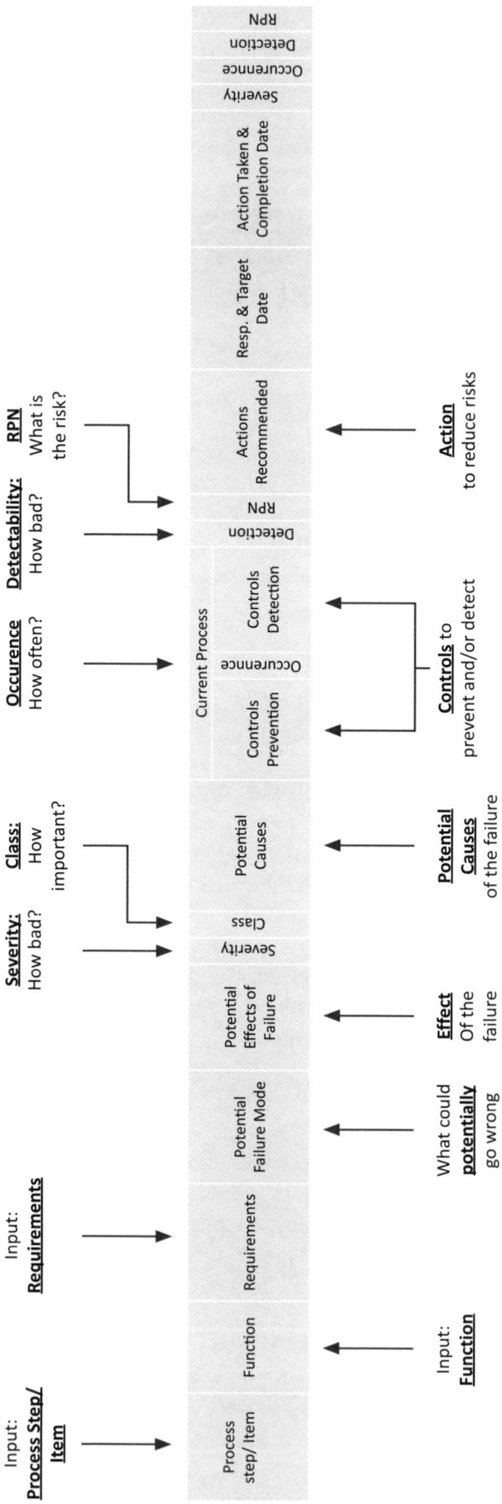

6

Figure 84 - *Failure Mode and Effect Analysis*

At step 11 the 'Risk Priority Number' (RPN) is calculated as the product of three quantitative ratings, which are related to the effects, causes, and controls. Based on the highest RPN scores, the team will start to determine action plans to decrease the RPNs.

1. Severity: the severity of the effect at the customer.
2. Occurrence: estimate the chance of failure occurrence.
3. Detection: how well can failures/causes be detected before they lead to the effect?

$$RPN = Severity \times Occurrence \times Detection$$

6.8.2 Control Plan

Another important FTR-tool is the Control plan which follows the steps of the process FMEA. The FMEA identifies what controls will be placed in the production process to catch any defects at various stages in the process. The Control plan provides more details on how the potential issues are checked. This can be applied to incoming quality, the assembly process and to end of line inspections of finished goods.

The Control plan is sometimes called an inspection plan and comprises all actions that should be performed to minimize or mitigate the potential failures as identified in the pFMEA. The Control plan should be a direct reflection of the pFMEA while the actions in the Control plan should be listed sequentially in the controls section of the pFMEA. The FMEA and the Control plan are two completely different tools, but they are linked by the process and by the controls.

Control actions include activities like set-up checks, measurements of components, amount of samples taken from the line for inspection, mistake proofing activities, the use of measurement equipment, statistical process control charts etc. The Control plan states who shall control what and how, how many and how often. This includes both product and process characteristics like equipment measures. The Control also states what need to be done if a so-called 'Out of Control situation' is observed. This is called the 'Out-of-Control Action Plan' (OCAP).

6

Figure 85 demonstrates an example of a Control Plan. Each of the columns is explained as well:

Part/ Process Number	Process Name/ Operation Description	Machine, Device, Jig, Tools, for Mfg.	Characteristic			Special Char Class	Methods					Reaction Plan
			No.	Product	Process		Product/ Process Specification/ Tolerance	Evaluation/ Measurement Technique	Size	Freq.	Control Method	

Figure 85 - *Control plan*

1. Location
   a. Process number.
   b. Process step description.
   c. Equipment needed.

2. Characteristic that needs to be inspected.
   a. Product, process or dimension.
   b. Severity Classification.

3. Method
   a. Specification.
   b. Measurement Gage.
   c. Size: Number of units to be inspected.
   d. Frequency: How often an inspection should occur.
   e. Measurement Method: How measurement needs to be performed and by whom.

4. OCAP / Reaction plan
   a. What needs to be done in case of an 'Out-of-Control' situation.

6

6.8.3 Jidoka & Poka Yoke

Poka Yoke is a Japanese term which means 'Mistake-proofing'. The concept of Poka Yoke was adopted by Shigeo Shingo in the 1960s to industrial processes designed to prevent human errors. It is one of the elements in the Toyota Production System. It was originally called 'Fool-proofing' or 'Idiot-proofing', but later on it was changed to be 'Mistake-proofing' to help focus on the process and maintain respect for the person.

Poka Yoke refers to any constraint designed into the process or product to prevent incorrect operation by the user. Its purpose is to eliminate product defects by preventing, correcting, or drawing attention to human errors as they occur. Originally it was applied in manufacturing processes where a physical feature is designed into the product or tooling to help an operator avoid (Yokeru) inadvertent errors (Poka). Examples can be found in everyday life like cable connectors which can only be mounted in one orientation. Another example would be an automatic transmission car that requires the gear lever to be in 'Park'-position before the key can be taken out. Also in transactional processes and healthcare examples of Poka Yoke can be found in forms, like the use of radio buttons, checklists and drop down menus instead of text fields to prevent entering incorrect data.

As most of the physical features have to be defined in the design phase, Poka Yoke is an important element in the design of new products.

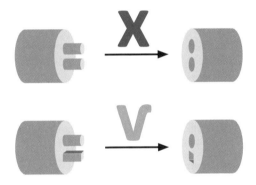

Figure 86 - *Poka Yoke example 1*

6

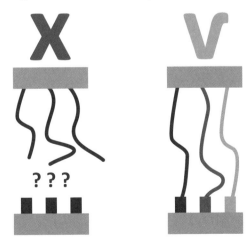

Figure 87 - *Poka Yoke example 2*

Jidoka is the principle that every person is authorized to stop the line when a quality problem occurs. Actually, it is each person's obligation to stop the line when he observes a problem. If a quality problem occurs, the Flow should be stopped and the issue should be resolved before the process can continue. This approach is an enabler to build-in quality at each process step rather than inspecting quality at the end of the line or putting parts aside when an abnormality occurs. If quality is inspected only at the end of the line, the problem will be detected much later and more products in between operation steps will contain the same quality problem.

Figure 88 - *Andon light*   **Figure 89** - *Emergency Stop*

Providing machines with the ability to detect abnormalities and immediately stop operations is called Autonomation. This is very often visualized by so-called 'Andon lights' at the top of a machine. Employees can stop the line by pulling a cord, called the 'Andon cord' or by pressing a red 'Stop button'. However, other ways can be applied as well like scanners, signatures or changing a status in an IT system.

Figure 90 - *Andon cord*

An example of applying Jidoka in an office environment is empowering hospital staff to stop the process if procedures aren't being followed, because continuing the treatment might harm the patient. Another example is to stop the process when a calculation mistake is discovered in the system. It should be repaired instead of being reworked over and over again.

Jidoka is one of the two pillars of the Toyota Production System along with Just In Time. It is an important principle to produce products and to deliver services First Time Right. However, many operation managers are scared of applying Jidoka across the entire operational process. Theoretically the line might be stopped every minute at a different operation step when a problem occurs, driving the total organization crazy and having not a single product delivered by the end of the day. This is indeed a big risk if the quality performance level is low at the different operation steps. The real meaning of Jidoka has been understood incorrectly for a long time by the Western world. To prevent this, the following three elements should be taken into account:

1 - Implement slowly
Start slowly, rather than stopping the line for every single abnormality from day one. Lines should be stopped for major problems and the organization should solve this problem and make sure it will not return again. Then slowly lowering the water level stop lines for smaller problems.

2 - Kaizen culture
Implementing Jidoka will not work if there is no culture for Continuous Improvement, if employees are lacking the skills of problem solving and if there is no structure or time for solving problems. A Kaizen Continuous Improvement culture and applying the problem solving tools as discussed in chapter 5 will be needed in order to implement Jidoka.

3 - Small buffers between lines
Applying Jidoka should be aligned with other Lean principles such as One-Piece Flow and Stock reduction between lines. If these principles are not aligned, there is a big risk of shutting down lines completely when an abnormality occurs. To avoid this, small buffers between lines or departments should be held to keep on running other part of the lines for a certain amount of time, while the abnormality is solved.

6

"Uncontrolled variation is

the enemy of quality."

- W. Edwards Deming -

7

CIMM Process Level IV Creating capable processes

The fourth level focuses on reducing variation in a stable process that is created in the first three levels. The objective is to increase the capability of the process performance. Rather than increasing quality with a step-by-step approach like the Kaizen approach, Six Sigma focuses on quality breakthrough improvement projects. A Six Sigma improvement project will take a few weeks or a few months rather than a few days. As a consequence the Six Sigma approach is much more top-down driven than the Kaizen bottom-up approach.

At this level we will apply Six Sigma and statistical tools, to analyze the performance of processes. In order to apply statistics, data will be needed. Therefore at this stage it is important to have a performance measurement system in place that is able to deliver process performance data at the level of the products or services that are produced. Green and Black Belts are expected to analyze the data by using statistical software like Minitab or other software. Most of the tools explained in this book, are demonstrated using Minitab. Yellow and Orange Belts are expected to understand and interpret many of these graphical outputs, but are not expected to generate them or to analyze the data.

A number of tools that can be used at this CIMM-level are presented in Table 7.1. It is important to realize that it is not necessary to use each of these tools in a Six Sigma project. The table only demonstrates tools that are commonly used. Other tools can be used as well. It is also important to realize that not each tool mentioned in this table is expected to be applied by Yellow and Orange Belts. Some tools are only applied at the level of Green and Black Belt. The roadmap used in this level is again the DMAIC approach. The tools listed in Table 7.1 are each placed in one of the DMAIC phases. However, many tools can be used in other phases as well.

7

Table 7.1. *Optional tools Level IV*

Define	Measure	Analyze	Improve	Control
Project Charter	Performance Metrics	Graphical Tools	Design of Experiments	First Time Right, Poka Yoke
Voice of Customer	Time Series Plot	Ishikawa	Reducing variation CTQ	FMEA, Control Plan
Costs of Poor Quality	Measurement System Analysis	Brainstorm Techniques	Reducing Muda (8 x Waste)	Training (Skill development)
SIPOC	Attribute Agreement Analysis	Hypothesis testing	Reducing Muri (Overburden)	Statistical Process Control
Pareto		Process Capability Analysis	Reducing Mura (Unevenness)	Auditing
CTQ Flowdown		Regression Analysis	Design for Excellence (DfX)	
Stakeholder Analysis				

7

Define

7.1 Critical to Quality (CTQ)

One of the first tools in the Define phase of a DMAIC project is that we have to compose a CTQ Flowdown based on the Voice of the Customer. We will explain this technique in the following sections. The CTQ will be our thread throughout the entire Lean Six Sigma project. Therefore it is an important element that we should work on very seriously.

7.1.1 Critical requirements

The Voice of Customer requirements are often expressed in an unclear manner. It is our task to interpret this into an unambiguous and measurable specification of the requirement. This metric is called the external Critical to Quality (CTQ_{ext}).

Projects are often linked to a particular area. Therefore the CTQ is sometimes called Critical to Safety (CTS), Critical to Process (CTP), Critical to Delivery (CTD) or Critical to Cost (CTC). In most cases however the measure is simply called 'Critical to Quality' (CTQ).

Figure 91 - *Voice of Customer VoC & External CTQ*

7.1.2 CTQ Flowdown

After defining the critical requirements from the customer, it is necessary to translate the external CTQ to an internal CTQ. The external CTQ is the metric that is related to the customers' requirement or complaint. The internal CTQ is the metric that is related to what we measure in our product or process to verify the quality of the product or service. Defining the proper CTQs is crucial for the Lean Six Sigma project because the CTQ_{int} becomes the thread throughout the entire Lean Six Sigma project. Focusing on an incorrect CTQ_{int} will result in a lot of effort but not in improved customer satisfaction.

- Define: The CTQ_{int} is the measurable characteristic that is representing the customers need.
- Measure: The CTQ_{int} should be measured properly and CTQ_{int} data should be available and reliable.
- Analyze: Potential factors of influence on the CTQ_{int} should be identified and investigated. The capability of the CTQ_{int} performance against the customer specifications should be analyzed.
- Improve: The negative effect of factors that have a significant influence on poor CTQ_{int} performance should be eliminated or decreased.
- Control: The improved performance of the CTQ_{int} should be verified and controlled.

A helpful tool for this is the CTQ Flowdown. A CTQ Flowdown represents the key measurable characteristics of a product or process whose performance standards or specification limits must be met in order to satisfy the customer requirements. The Lean Six Sigma project is focusing on a limited number of CTQ_{int}s, ideally even a single CTQ_{int} and improvement effort or design effort should still be aligned to these measurable customer requirements. Although this tool looks very simple, setting up a proper CTQ Flowdown can be a very complicated team effort.

The effort of decomposing the VOC to a lower level should focus on responses and not on defining the factors of influence. This will be done later in the DMAIC project. In problem solving, the response is called 'Y' and the factors of influence 'X'. Finally we need to define how we are going to measure the CTQ_{int}. We call this the Operational Definition of the CTQ_{int}. This definition consists of all of the following:

1. The characteristic of the product / service to be measured.
    The 'hard' (measurable) metric of the 'soft' CTQ description.

2. The measurement procedure.
    Includes the instrument that is used and data collection procedure to follow.

3. The requirements on the CTQ_{int}.
    The specification for the measure that determines (without discussion) if the VOC is met or not.

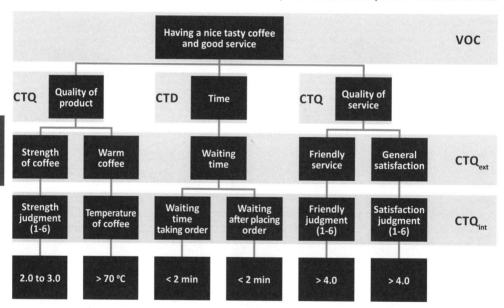

Figure 92 - Example CTQ Flowdown coffee bar

Measure

7.2 Six Sigma performance metrics

Determining the quality of the measurement system and the data acquired are the heart of any DMAIC improvement process. It is decided what CTQ_{int} should be measured and how it is measured. The CTQ_{int} should be measured properly and CTQ_{int} data should be available and reliable. Since many tools in the Measure and Analyze phase work with data, it is necessary to know how to qualify poor quality.

7.2.1 Defects and Defectives

There are two different ways to indicate that a product is 'bad'. First, you can say that the product is 'Defective'. This indicates that something is wrong with the product. It does not work as it is supposed to, or it does not look like it is supposed to. The product does not meet the specifications or expectations of the customer. Second, the defective product can have one or multiple 'Defects'. In this case a single product has more than one dimensions or features that are out of specification or expectation. Examples are several typing mistakes in one document, multiple dimensions out of specification for one component, several scratches on one product, etc.

In summary, it only takes one 'Defect' to create one 'Defective' product. However, one 'Defective' product can have several 'Defects'. The difference is important for yield calculations as explained in the following sections. To quantify the quality level of a process the following metrics are used:

1. ppm: Parts per Million.
2. DPU: Defects per Unit.
3. DPMO: Defects per Million Opportunities.
4. Yield: Percentage of good products.
5. Rolled throughput Yield (RTY): Probability a unit will pass a number of sequential process steps without any defect.

1 - ppm (Parts per Million):
In high volume operations with high demand for quality, the ppm measure is used to indicate the quality performance of a production process. The abbreviation stands for defective parts per million. Example: 50 ppm performance indicates that within a production volume of one million parts, it is expected to find 50 products that do not meet specifications. If 100,000 parts are produced, a 50 ppm performance means that it is expected that 5 parts do not meet the specification. For many operations 50 ppm is already a pretty high quality standard to meet, but a Six Sigma performance is expecting an even higher quality performance of 3.4 ppm [see section 7.8.4].

2 - DPU (Defects per Unit):
A defect is defined as a non-conformance of a quality characteristic to its specification. DPU is the total number of defects per unit. DPU can be greater than 1 because one unit can have several defects (e.g. a hood of a car can contain multiple dents or scratches and a document can contain more than one typing mistake).

7

3 - DPMO (Defects per Million Opportunities):

The abbreviation DPMO stands for Defects Per Million Opportunities or nonconformities per million opportunities. DPMO is similar to ppm and is used as a quality performance measure. However, DPMO differs from ppm in that it comprehends the possibility that one unit under inspection may be found to have multiple defects of the same type or may have multiple types of defects.

The measure DPMO can also be used to compare the quality performance of different products. Using the DPMO measure we can for instance compare the quality performance of a computer with a toaster. The computer has much more opportunities to fail than the toaster, because the computer is more complex and it consist of more components than the toaster.

4 - Process Yield (%):

Yield is the percentage of good products that are passed to the next operation. This can best be explained by an example. Assume we are producing a part of a toaster in 4 consecutive process steps (A, B, C and D). Each process step delivers a number of good parts (Out) and a number of bad parts (Scrap). Any part that contains a fault that can be successfully reworked is counted as a good part. Any part that contains a fault that cannot be successfully reworked clearly is counted as a bad part. All the good parts go to the next process step and the bad parts have to be thrown away.

$$Process\ Yield\ [\%] = \frac{Total\ number\ of\ products\ without\ defects}{Total\ number\ of\ products}$$

You can find the process Yield [%] of each of the four process steps in Table 7.2.

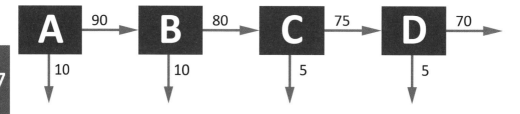

Table 7.2. *Process Yield*

Process	Scrap	Out						Yield-%
A	10	90	90 / (90+10)	=	90 /100	=	90%	
B	10	80	80 / (80+10)	=	80 / 90	=	89%	
C	5	75	75 / (75+5)	=	75 / 80	=	94%	
D	5	70	70 / (70+5)	=	70 / 75	=	93%	
Total							70%	

$Process\ Yield = 0.90 \times 0.89 \times 0.94 \times 0.93 = 70\%$

5 - Rolled Throughput Yield (RTY%):

In many cases the Rolled Throughput Yield (RTY%) or First Time Right Yield (FTR%) is used rather than the Process Yield. The 'Rolled Throughput Yield' is defined as the probability that a unit will pass a number of sequential process steps without any defect. The main difference between RTY and normal Process Yield, is that products that are not 100% OK, but could be reworked or corrected, are now considered incorrect in the RTY-calculation, because the products were not 'Right the First Time'.

Rolled Throughput Yield helps us measure the cumulative effects of inefficiencies found throughout the process. It can be calculated by the product of yields for each process step of the entire process:

$$Rolled\ Throughput\ Yield\ [\%] = \frac{Total\ number\ of\ products\ right\ first\ time}{Total\ number\ of\ products}$$

We will explain this once again with an example:

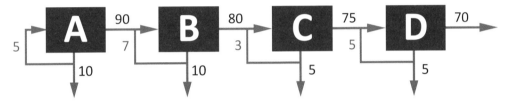

Table 7.3. *Rolled Throughput Yield*

Process	Scrap	Rework	Out			FTR-%
A	10	5	90	(90-5) / (90+10) =	85 /100	= 85%
B	10	7	80	(80-7) / (80+10) =	73 / 90	= 81%
C	5	3	75	(75-3) / (75+5) =	72 / 80	= 90%
D	5	5	70	(70-5) / (70+5) =	65 / 75	= 87%
RTY-%						54%

$$RTY = 0.85 \times 0.81 \times 0.90 \times 0.87 = 54\%$$

Each of the process steps have a number of OK parts that are passed on to the next operation, but some of these products have been reworked, repaired or corrected. Taking into account that some of the products were not OK the first time, the Rolled Throughput Yield of this process is 54%.

7.2.2 Sampling methods

Preparing samples, shutting down a line to perform a test and the amount of effort that people put into performing the test is expensive. Therefore, proper preparation is needed. A data collection plan should be composed in advance that already includes the numbered samples and columns specifying the data that need to be collected. The preparation should also include a number of test samples that can be used to set up the tooling and to evaluate the measurement procedure itself before the start of the actual data collection effort. Changing tooling, samples or procedure after you have started the measurement procedure, can invalidate the entire test.

For service organizations with system data it is important to be clear on what database and time period the data should be collected from. Proper time should be spent to define what data should be taken from the business system. First, if you decide that data about 'waiting times' should be collected, it is important to decide the start and end point that defines 'waiting time'. Second, you should make sure this data are actually available in the system and can be exported or extracted from the system. Collecting the wrong data is a Waste in itself and can result in erroneous conclusions and subsequently lead to the wrong actions being taken.

The total collection of objects is called the 'Population'. Only when all objects of the population are measured, the true mean and standard deviation can be known. Generally it is not realistic to measure all objects of the population. Fortunately it is not necessary to measure the entire population. If we apply statistics in a proper way, a subset or 'Sample' of the population can be used. When sampling data, it is always important to achieve a representative sample that is an accurate, proportional depiction of the population under study.

7.2.3 Data collection tools

There are various data collection tools that might be used by Yellow and Orange Belts:

1 - Data sheet:
A data sheet is used to capture numerical readings, measures or counts. There is usually some unique identifier in the left hand column with all required measurements recorded to the right.

2 - Check sheet:
Check sheets are often used to collect data about defects or causes of defects [5.2.2]. Possible causes are listed on a sheet and a tick is made for every occurrence. After a set period of time, the checks can be counted to provide a summary.

3 - Concentration diagram:
A concentration diagram uses a picture or diagram of the product or document on which the location of defects/problems/damage are then marked by the observer. Examples of concentration diagrams are registering data on rental car damage, plastic molding defects and errors on forms.

4 - Questionnaire or survey:
Questionnaires or surveys use carefully scripted questions with a discrete set of responses for respondents to choose from.

7.3 Statistics

Statistics is the study of the collection, organization, analysis, interpretation and presentation of data. Statistics deals with all aspects of data including the planning and execution of experiments, the collection of data and the analysis of the data. In this section we will review the aspects of special cause variation and common cause variation. We will also review the basic terms of sample and descriptive statistics.

7.3.1 Descriptive statistics

Descriptive statistics is a set of measures (statistics) that characterizes a given set of data, which can either be a representation of the entire population or a sample. Based on the sample we can calculate statistics to estimate parameters of the whole population. These statistics of the sample are always estimates with quantifiable confidence.

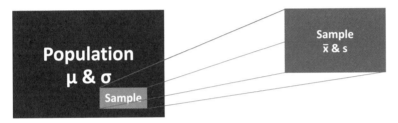

Figure 93 - *Population and Sample*

Process data have several components:

- Center   Is the process on target?
- Spread   How much variation is in the data?
- Shape   What does the shape of the distribution look like?
- Stability   Does the process drift in time?

Measures of Central Tendency
The center of the process is called Central Tendency. There are different measures for Central Tendency. Which measure to use depends on the objective of the analysis and the shape of the population. Usually, especially for the Normal distribution and other symmetrical distributed populations, the 'Mean' is used. The symbol 'μ' (mu) represents the Mean of a population, while '$\bar{x}$' (Xbar) represents the Mean of a sample.

Below, three measures of Central Tendency are listed based on a simple set of data: {3, 5, 4, 7, 5}.

Mean:
Arithmetic Mean of data

$$\bar{x} = \frac{(3+5+4+7+5)}{5} = 4.8$$

Median:
Middle value of sorted data (for uneven sample size)
Mean of the middlemost values (for even sample size)

$$Median(3;4;5;5;7) = 5$$

Mode:
Most common value in the data set

$$Mode(3;4;5;5;7) = 5$$

Measures of Spread
Also for the spread within the sample data there are different measures. Which measure is used depends again on the objective of the analysis and the data. The symbol 'σ' (sigma) represents the Standard Deviation of a population, while 's' represents the Standard Deviation of a sample.

Range (R):
Absolute difference between maximum
and minimum value of the data set

$$R = x_{max} - x_{min}$$

Interquartile Range (IQR):
Range of inner 50% of the data set

$$IQR = x_{75\%} - x_{25\%}$$

Variance (s²) of a sample:
Average of the squared deviations from $\bar{x}$
(Divided by n-1 to get an unbiased estimator)

$$s^2 = \frac{1}{n-1}\sum_{i=1}^{n}\left(x_i - \bar{x}\right)^2$$

Standard Deviation (SD) or (s):
Square root of the variance s²

$$s = \sqrt{s^2}$$

Measures for both central tendency, standard deviation and variance can be generated respectively in Excel by using the functions '=AVERAGE', '=STDEV' and '=VAR' on the set of data. Within Lean Six Sigma Green and Black Belts often use Minitab to calculate descriptive statistic.

7

7.3.2 Variation

Variation is everywhere. A driver has variation when parking his car; the arrival times of trains have variation; the human race shows enormous variation and products extracted out of a process are never the same. Every process demonstrates variation. The less variation a process has, the better we can predict its outcome. Therefore Lean Six Sigma has a strong focus on reducing variation. If we want to base our decisions within problem solving projects on facts, we have to know how to analyze and interpret data. In this section we will review how to analyze the two main characteristics of a set of data: the center (e.g. mean) and spread (e.g. standard deviation).

The difference between the so-called 'Old view' of variation and the 'Modern view' of variation is shown in Figure 94. The old approach is about approving the product when it meets the specification and rejecting the product when it does not meet the specification. There were only good and bad products. A much better way of looking at products meeting specification is to realize that a product that is exactly in the middle of the specifications is better than a product that is very close to one of its specification limits. Furthermore, a process that demonstrates little variation is better than a process that demonstrates a lot of variation.

Old view

Modern view

Figure 94 - *Quality (Old view versus Modern view)*

Process stability, reducing variation and improving process capability are important concepts of the Six Sigma methodology. Solving instabilities can often be done by performing Kaizen and Lean initiatives, without the use of comprehensive statistical analysis, while Six Sigma initiatives focus on centering the process (Mean), reducing process variation (Spread) and improving process capability. There are two types of variation that cause a process to perform at an inadequate level:

1. Special cause variation
2. Common cause variation

It is important to distinguish between both types of variation, so that a suitable intervention can be applied. In process improvement initiatives it is recommended to focus on solving special cause variation prior to common cause variation, because normally the reasons for special cause variation are found more easily than the reasons for common cause variation.

Special cause variation
Special cause variation is caused by factors that result in a non-random distribution of the output. Special cause variation is a shift or a sudden change, caused by an incident or certain change in surroundings. Special cause variation is also called exceptional or assignable variation. A process that has special cause variation is called "Out-of-control '.

Figure 95 demonstrates that process 'A' has very little natural variation, but the process demonstrates special cause variation. The graph does not clarify the reason for that, but by making this graph and discussing it with people involved can generate hypotheses about the reasons. Possible reasons may be a door slamming, a loose tooling, a component damaged, dirt or an employee who makes a mistake due to lack of sleep. Within Lean Six Sigma these improvement possibilities are considered as 'Low hanging fruit' initiatives, since the causes are often readily apparent.

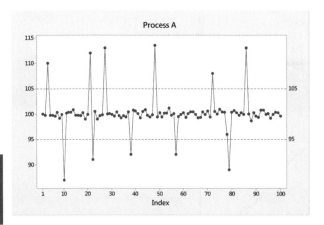

Figure 95 - *Special Cause variation*

As an example we will demonstrate the verification process of an electronic sensor, with a specification for Voltage of 3.5±1.0[V]. The process demonstrates a Yield of 94% and 6% Yield loss. The sensors are measured four pieces simultaneously in a fixture. We generate a 'Times Series Plot' for 100 measurements. Figure 96 demonstrates six outliers with an extreme value of 0 [V]. By using the 'Brush' option in Minitab we can visualize the available variables, like the number of the fixture that is part of the data set. This demonstrates that all six outliers came from the same fixture (Nr. 3). After detailed investigation it turned out the reason for the outliers was a bad electrical contact. Further investigation proved that the underlying root cause appeared to be an incorrect preparation of the fixture.

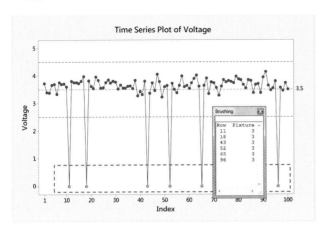

Figure 96 - *Extreme Special Cause variation*

Special cause variation is not always extreme, but sometimes less obvious. Figure 97 demonstrates that process 'B' shows little natural variation, but suddenly the Mean of the process has shifted. Possible reasons for this behavior might be the use of different components, different suppliers, different operators, different set-up or different machines.

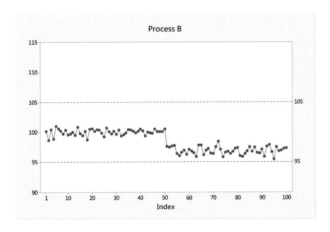

Figure 97 - *Special Cause variation*

7

Common Cause Variation

Common cause variation is caused by the process itself. Every process has some amount of fluctuation caused by unknown factors, resulting in a steady but random distribution of output around the average of the data. Common cause variation is a measure of the process potential or process technology. Common cause variation is the remaining variation after removing instabilities and special cause variation. This type of variation is also called natural variation, random variation, noise, non-controllable variation, inherent variation or within-subgroup variation. If a process shows only natural variation it is in a state of statistical control.

In Figure 98 and Figure 99 two Time Series plots are shown. You can see that process 'C' has relatively little variation compared to process 'D', but both processes demonstrate a stable process with only common cause variation. A process showing only Common Cause Variation is 'Stable', 'Predictable' and 'In-Control'. Yet, it does not mean that the results will automatically match the quality standards required. It only means that the results are stable and predictable.

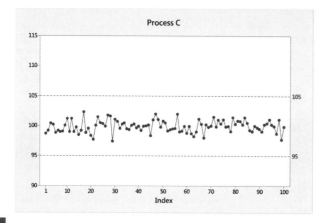

Figure 98 - *Common Cause variation*

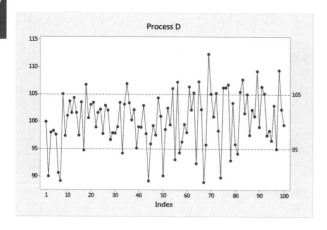

Figure 99 - *Common Cause variation*

Table 7.4. *Examples of different types of variation (Industry)*

Instability	Special Cause	Common Cause
Quality spill (incident)	Performance varies from day to day	Natural variation
Missing O-ring	O-rings from this bag are more difficult to mount	Some O-rings are tighter than other
No electrical contact	Different fixtures have different resistance	Natural process variation (of resistance)
Damaged components	Some boxes demonstrate more variability than others	Differences from one component to the other
Lead time for rush order	Lead time for changing work load	Lead time for fixed workload

Table 7.5. *Examples of different types of variation (Transactional)*

Instability	Special Cause	Common Cause
Doctor is called for emergency	Waiting time on Monday is longer than on Friday	Natural variation of Waiting time during a day
Forgot to call back a client	No time today. We will call him back tomorrow!	Response time in normal operation
Email sent to incorrect person	Answering 200 mails after returning from holiday	Answering about 50 mails each day
Missing signature or approval	Response time Manager A is different than Manager B	Response time of Manager A
Late delivery caused by accident	Longer travel times during rush hours	Average speed on highway

7

7.4 Distributions

7.4.1 Continuous distributions

For calculating probabilities it is important to know how to apply probability distributions. The Normal probability distribution is well-known, but there are also other types of probability distributions. In this chapter we will review one of the most common continuous distributions, called the Normal distribution. Yellow Belts are expected to recognize the Normal distribution plot, while Orange Belts are expected to understand and interpret the Normal distribution.

Normal distribution

There are many different types of distributions, but the Normal distribution (or Gaussian distribution) is the most common statistical distribution. This is because normality arises naturally in many physical measurements (e.g. dimensions of produced products, temperature), biological measurements (e.g. body temperature, length of bones) and social measurements (e.g. media campaign responses, number of tweets, IQ).

The Normal distribution is bell-shaped. Normal distributions are characterized as $N(\mu;\sigma)$, where μ is the population mean and σ is the population standard deviation. The amount of data at a certain distance from the Mean can be defined as follows:

About 68.3% of the data within the population is within $\mu \pm 1\sigma$.
About 95.4% of the data within the population is within $\mu \pm 2\sigma$.
About 99.7% of the data within the population is within $\mu \pm 3\sigma$.

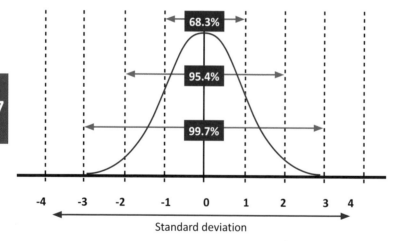

Figure 100 - *Normal distribution and Standard deviation*

The so-called Standard Normal Distribution is characterized as N(0;1) with a mean μ = 0 and standard deviation σ = 1.

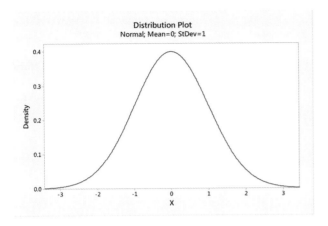

Figure 101 - *Normalized distribution plot*

7.4.2 Discrete distributions

In this section we will review Bernoulli trials and two discrete distributions: the Poisson and Binomial distribution. Yellow Belts are not expected to understand these discrete distributions, while Orange Belts are expected to remember the Poisson and Binomial distribution. They are not expected to reproduce the calculations that are explained in the following sections.

Bernoulli trials

A Bernoulli trial is a random experiment with exactly two possible outcomes: 'Success' and 'Failure'. The outcome is binary. The probability of success is the same every time the experiment is conducted and is represented by P(Success) = p. The probability of a failure is given by P(Failure) = 1 - P(Success). A common example of a Bernoulli trial is flipping a coin. Instead of 'Success' and 'Failure', you can also use '1' and '0':

- $P(1) = p$
- $P(0) = 1 - p$

The Binomial distribution is a discrete probability distribution of the number of successes in a sequence of mutually independent Bernoulli trials, each with the same probability of success. In the case of flipping a coin there are exactly two outcomes. With a fair coin you have a probability of 50% to observe 'Heads'; (p = 0.5) and 50% to observe 'Tails'; (1 - p = 0.5).

Another example is rolling a dice. Assume we define 'a six' as 'Success' and the complementary event 'not a six' as 'Failure'. Since there are six outcomes the chance of success P(6) = 0.167. The chance of getting 1 through 5 is 1 - p = 1 - 0.167 = 0.833.

In both examples the probability of the outcome of a trial does not depend on previous outcomes. If we flip the coin 5 times, and would like to know the probability of getting 'Heads' five times in a row: P(5x Heads) = p^5 = (0.5)^5 = 0.0312.

Binomial distribution

Assume we are interested in our chances of observing 'Head' ten times in a row when flipping a coin 100 times, or observing '6' three times, when we roll the dice 20 times. These type of questions can be answered by looking at a Binomial distribution. The probability distribution of X is called a Binomial distribution with n Bernoulli trials and probability of Success $P(X=Success) = p$.

Assume we roll a dice 20 times and we would like to know the probability of observing three times '6'. Applying statistical software, Green and Black Belts can calculate the probability for a series of number of successes. This will result in a so called distribution plot of the Binomial distribution as shown in Figure 102.

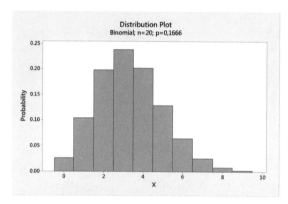

Figure 102 - *Binomial distribution plot*

Poisson distribution

The Poisson distribution is a discrete probability distribution. This distribution expresses the probability of a given number of events occurring in a fixed interval of time or the number of defects that occur in a unit or product. The occurrence of events or defects are mutually independent. The Poisson distribution can be used for the number of events per interval (e.g. time, area, volume).

Example: The average number of incidents in a weekend is '6'. What is the probability that in the next weekend '3' incidents occur? Green and Black Belts are able to answer these type of questions by using the Poisson distribution. The probability distribution plot is demonstrated in Figure 103.

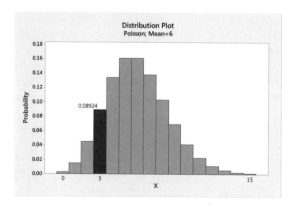

Figure 103 - *Poisson distribution plot*

7.5 Measurement Systems

Metrology is the 'science of measurement', and includes a number of theoretical and practical aspects of the measurement process. It is important to ensure that data which are used in an improvement project are valid and reliable. For this purpose, it is necessary that use a reliable measurement system which, moreover, has sufficient resolution. This is one of the key elements of a Lean Six Sigma project because conclusions based on unreliable data are unreliable themselves. Therefore, much attention is given in the Measure-phase of a DMAIC project to the evaluation of the measurement system.

7.5.1 Measurement Methods

There are many different measurement tools. One example is the so-called 'Go / No Go Gage' (Figure 104) which is used to assess whether an item meets a certain specification or tolerance. The Gage has two possible outcomes: OK (approval) or NOK (rejection). The use of this type of Gages is based on the principle of Poka Yoke, because the outcome is not open to interpretation. Standard 'Go / No Go Gages' can be purchased from various suppliers, but sometimes such Gage is tailormade to evaluate a specific component or assembly. Another example of a measurement system is the caliper, shown in Figure 105.

Figure 104 - *Go/No go Gages*

7

Figure 105 - *Measurement system: Caliper*

In addition to the measurement tool itself, also the measurement method or measurement process is of great importance for carrying out a proper measurement. When you perform a number of consecutive measurements you do not necessarily always get the same value. For example, step on a scale to measure your weight. You will probably get a slightly different value each time. This measurement variation is part of the measurement system. 'How important is this variation?' and 'Is this variation small enough to draw conclusions about the performance?' In the following sections we will discuss the measurement system as a whole, consisting both of the measuring instrument and the measurement process.

7.5.2 Measurement System Analysis (MSA)

Every measurement instrument shows variation. Besides the variation of the instrument, there are other sources of variation, for example:

- Operators performing the measurements.
- Operating procedures.
- Data collection forms.
- Tools and aids that are used.
- The way and frequency samples are taken from the line.
- Calibration technique.
- Environment (temperature, moisture, vibration, light, etc.).
- . . .

The ideal measurement system produces the true value every time. However . . . we all know nothing is perfect! Just like any other process, the collection of data and performing measurements on the product is a process in itself. Obtaining data and doing measurements will demonstrate variability and produce defects.

We will review how a 'Measurement System Analysis' (MSA) is performed on the measurement system. The MSA tells you how precise the measurement tool is (the equipment) and how large the impact of the measurement process is (e.g. operator and procedure). An MSA evaluates the test method, measuring instruments, and the entire process of obtaining measurements in order to quantify measurement accuracy and variability. This is important for making decisions about a product or process.

The process variation that we observe by reading the measurement data on the instrument, is always larger than the actual process variation. This is because we have to take the variation caused by the Measurement System (Gage) into account. The 'Observed variation' is also called the 'Total variation'. The actual 'Process variation' is also called 'Part-to-Part variation'.

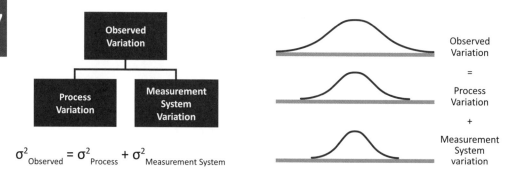

$$\sigma^2_{Observed} = \sigma^2_{Process} + \sigma^2_{Measurement\ System}$$

Figure 106 - *Observed variation and Measurement system variation*

To minimize measurement system variation, it is important to identify and understand the factors of influence. Measurement system errors can be characterized into the following three categories:

A. Accuracy: How big is the systematic error?
    1. Bias:
        The difference between the measured average and the true value.
    2. Linearity:
        Equal accuracy over the entire range of the instrument.

B. Precision: How big is the measurement variation?
    1. Repeatability:
        The amount of variation that is caused by the measuring instrument itself.
    2. Reproducibility:
        The amount of variation that is caused by the measurement procedure, operator, etc.
    3. Uniformity:
        Extent to which measurement variation is constant (uniform) over the whole range of the measurement scale.

C. Stability: Is the measurement system stable over time?

If you ask someone how good a measurement system is, he might tell you 'It has been calibrated recently, so it is perfect'. Keep in mind that calibration of the system is only one aspect of a good measurement system. A calibrated system is no guarantee for Accuracy, Precision or for Stability. An MSA is always done in combination with the objects to be measured.

| Accurate | + | Precise | = | Perfection |

Figure 107 - *Measurement system variation*

7

1 - Accuracy

The accuracy of a measurement system is also called the systematic difference between the measured average and the true value or Bias. Bias effects include:

Employee Bias:
Several employees get different measurement averages for the same object. Also different observations, or retrieving data from different database systems will cause this type of error. A effective measurement instruction, training and clear definitions will limit the extent of Employee Bias.

Instrument Bias:
Several instruments get different measurement averages for the same object. This can be minimized by performing calibration of the Gage. Realize however that the Bias after the calibration process will be determined by the reference value that is used for the calibration process.

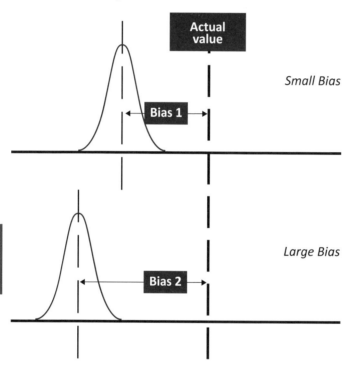

Figure 108 - *Measurement system Accuracy (Bias)*

2 - Precision (Repeatability & Reproducibility)

Precision is the total amount of variation of the measurement system. This includes variation caused by the measurement instrument and the measurement process. The amount of Precision variability can be determined by a Measurement System Analysis (Gage R&R), where the two Rs stand for Repeatability and Reproducibility.

Repeatability is the proportion of the inherent variation that is caused by the measuring instrument itself, also called 'test-retest error'. It is the variation which occurs when repeated measurements are taken on the same object without changing the circumstances (e.g. same employee, same samples, same set-up, same measurement instrument, short time period, etc.).

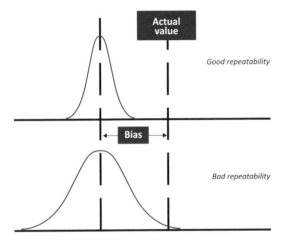

Figure 109 - *Measurement system precision (Repeatability)*

Reproducibility is the variation caused by the measurement procedure. This is the variation that occurs when repeated measurements are made of the same object under different conditions (e.g. different operators or employee, different set-ups, different test units, different environmental conditions, long time period).

7

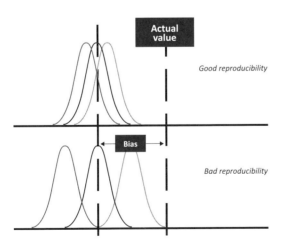

Figure 110 - *Measurement system precision (Reproducibility)*

Analyze

7.6 Hypothesis Testing and Confidence Intervals

The objective of Six Sigma is to reduce the variation of the CTQ by identifying the root causes of the variation and eliminate the root causes or reduce their influences. To identify and verify the root causes we have at our disposal different statistical methods. Most of them are using Hypothesis testing. Hypothesis tests are used to test statements about a population. Confidence intervals are used to quantify the confidence of the estimates of the population parameters.

7.6.1 Hypothesis testing

Hypothesis testing is used to investigate if a statement is 'True' or 'False'. For example if we want to investigate if a certain factor has an influence on the process, we start by defining the null hypothesis (H_0) and the alternative hypothesis (H_A). There is a special way of formulating the hypotheses, which is often compared with a lawsuit where a suspect is still innocent until the opposite is proven. The starting point in hypothesis testing therefore is always that we assume there is no influence, even when we suspect that there actually is an influence. The null hypothesis is always defined as 'there is no influence of factor X' or 'there is no difference between machine A and machine B', etc. The alternative hypothesis then describes the difference. This however is an assumption that must be investigated and proven.

For many people, defining the hypothesis is confusing in the beginning, so let's illustrate it with an example. Suppose we suspect that Machine A produces bars that are longer than the bars produced by Machine B. The null hypothesis needs to be defined as 'Bars produced by Machine A are of equal length as bars produced by Machine B'. Keep in mind that 'One is presumed innocent until proven guilty'.

- H_0: Bars produced by Machine A have equal length to bars produced by Machine B.
- H_A: Bars produced by Machine A are longer than bars produced by Machine B.

The next step is to investigate the length of bars produced by Machine A and compare it with the length of the bars produced by Machine B. 'Hypothesis testing' covers a range of statistical tests that are applied by Green and Black Belts to investigate data and to reach decisions.

Based on the hypothesis, we predict the outcome of the test. This again can be compared with a lawsuit. Even if there is hard evidence and the suspect is found guilty, the truth might be that the person is not guilty at all. Once in a while such stories will get into the news. In statistical terms we will call this conclusion a 'Type I Error'. The other possibility is that a person who is found not guilty by the jury, is actually guilty. A guilty person who is free to go, is called a 'Type II Error' in statistical terms. Evidently, we try our best to keep these two types of errors as small as possible. To accomplish this we need as much evidence we can get. In statistics this means more samples and more data. But whatever 'evidence' we have, we need to realize that 100% certainty is not possible within statistics.

The 'Type-I Error' is the situation that we reject the null hypothesis although we should not. The significance level or alpha level 'α' is the probability of rejecting the null hypothesis when the null hypothesis is actually true. The 'Type-II error' is the situation that we accept the null hypothesis when this hypothesis is not true. The probability of this error is called Beta or 'β'.

- Type-I error: Supporting the alternate hypothesis when the null hypothesis is true.
- Type-II error: Not supporting the alternate hypothesis when the alternate hypothesis is true.

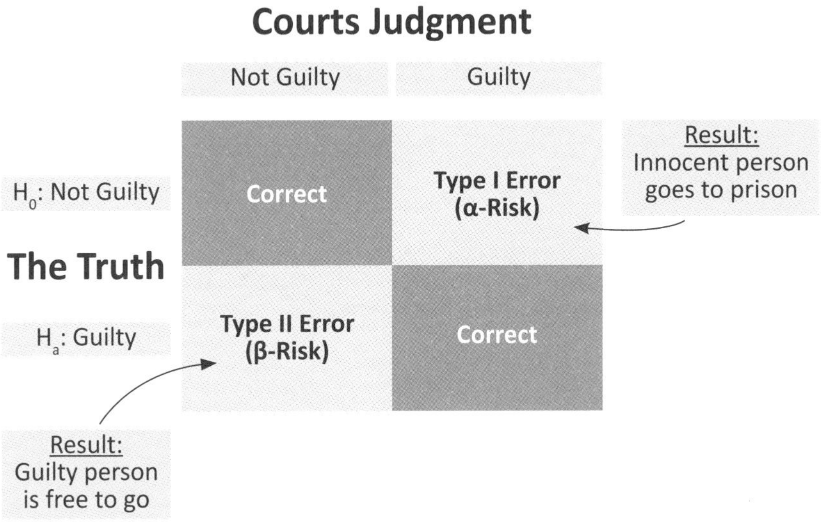

Courts Judgment

	Not Guilty	Guilty	
H_0: Not Guilty	Correct	Type I Error (α-Risk)	Result: Innocent person goes to prison
The Truth			
H_a: Guilty	Type II Error (β-Risk)	Correct	

Result: Guilty person is free to go

Figure 111 - *Confidence Interval - Type I and Type II error*

7.6.2 Confidence Intervals

Statistics such as the average ($\overline{X}$) and standard deviation (s) of the sample are only estimates, not the actual values of the population parameters! From sample to sample these estimates will differ. A so-called 'Confidence Interval' (CI) indicates how reliable our estimate is. Unless we investigate the entire population, we have to accept that we can never be 100% sure about our estimates.

Instead of assuming a statistic is absolutely accurate, Confidence Intervals can be used to provide a range within which the true process statistic is likely to be with a known level of confidence. The confidence level defines how sure we are of conclusions that are drawn. Often a 95% level of confidence is used, but we can choose other levels. If we want to be more confident, we would need to increase the sample size.

Assume we want to draw a sample to calculate a 95% Confidence Interval for a population parameter. Then there is a 95% probability that the Confidence Interval will contain the actual value of the parameter. In other words: when we draw a large number of samples, about 95% of the calculated Confidence Intervals will contain the actual value of the parameter. It does not mean that the parameter's actual value has a probability of 95% of lying within the Confidence Interval.

Alpha levels are related to Confidence Intervals. You can choose the alpha level yourself. To define the alpha level, you have to subtract your Confidence Interval from 1. For example, if you want to be 95% confident that your analysis is correct, the alpha level would be $1 - 0.95 = 0.05$ which is 5%, assuming that you had a one tailed test. For two-tailed tests you have to divide the alpha level by 2. In this example, the two tailed alpha would be $5\% / 2 = 2.5\%$, as shown in Figure 112.

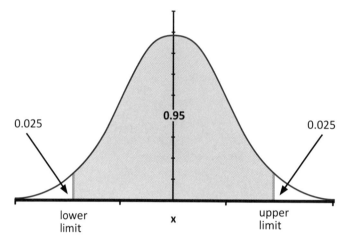

Figure 112 - *Confidence Interval - Alpha levels*

Even some experienced Green and Black Belts have difficulty of understanding the meaning of hypothesis testing, confidence intervals and alpha levels. Yellow and Orange Belts are expected to understand the basic principles of hypothesis testing and confidence intervals. It is important to understand that in statistics we can never be 100% sure about our conclusions, but that increasing the sample size will reduce the chance of drawing the incorrect conclusions (Type I or Type II error).

7.6.3 Sample size
It is seldom possible to investigate the complete population because the population is too large to measure all objects or the population only partially exists (e.g. production process). Therefore we want to estimate the parameters of the population instead. To do this we need a sample, a subset from the population. As mentioned Hypothesis tests are used to test statements about the population. Confidence intervals are used to quantify the confidence of the estimates of the population parameters.

The sample size has a big impact on the confidence of the outcome. The sample size of the population has a big influence on the confidence of statistical conclusions. Yellow and Orange Belts should recall that a larger sample size will increase the confidence of testing, but will increase the time and costs of the experiments. Calculation of the optimal sample size is pretty complicated and is often done by Green or Black Belts.

7.7 Correlation and Regression

'Correlation and Regression' is an approach for analyzing data and summarizing their main characteristics. This includes descriptive statistics and visualization of data. In this section we will review a number of additional techniques that are typically used in the Analyze phase of the DMAIC approach. Yellow Belts are expected to understand the basics of linear regression and correlation coefficient, while Orange Belts are also expected to apply regression models for estimation and prediction, and to interpret the correlation coefficient.

7.7.1 Correlation Coefficient

Correlation Analysis studies the degree of correlation between two continuous variables. It should be noted that a Correlation does not necessarily mean that there is a cause and effect relation. The Pearson Correlation Coefficient is used to measure the strength of the linear relationship between two variables. The correlation coefficient assumes a value between -1 and +1.

- '-1'   Depicts complete inverse (negative) dependence.
- '0'   Depicts complete independence.
- '+1'   Depicts complete direct (positive) dependence.

The following general rules can be applied to determine the strength of a correlation:

- Strong: Correlation Coefficient $|R| > 0.8$
- Moderate: Correlation Coefficient $0.5 < |R| < 0.8$
- Weak: Correlation Coefficient $|R| < 0.5$

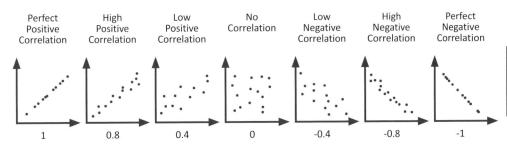

Figure 113 - *Pearson Correlation Coefficients*

7.7.2 Regression Analysis

Regression Analysis investigates the Cause and Effect relationship of a Factor on a Response. The 'Response' is the dependent variable Y, that changes as a result of a changing 'Factor'. The 'Factor' is the independent variable X, also called the Predictor variable. The predictor variables can be both continuous and categorical. Linear Regression generates an equation that describes the linear (statistical) relationship between a continuous response variable and one or more predictor variables. Regression models can be used to interpolate. They can also be used to extrapolating, but this is risky.

Example: assume your hobby is gardening and you are interested in the relationship between growth of plants (height) and time (weeks). Over a period of time you collect the data as listed in Table 7.6.

Table 7.6. *Growth of plants*

Week:	2	4	6	8	10	12	14	16	18
Height [cm]:	4	14	27	36	45	62	67	83	94

Using statistical software, you will be able to determine the Pearson correlation and the regression equation of Week and Height. The equation can be graphically represented by a simple linear fitted line plot:

- Pearson correlation: $R = 0.998$ (very strong)
- Regression equation: Height = -8.08 + 5.608 x Week

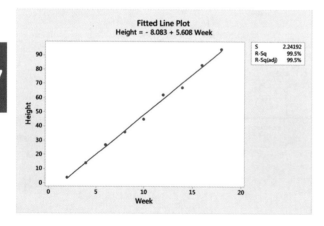

Figure 114 - *Linear Regression analysis plot*

7.8 Process Capability and Performance

When discussing process capability, two somewhat contrasting concepts need to be considered: 'Process Capability' and 'Process Performance'. Process capability shows what the process can do and process performance is what the process is actually doing. The gap between these two concepts can be seen as an opportunity for improvement. Yellow and Orange Belts are expected to understand the basic principles of process capability studies and to understand the difference between long-term and short-term capability. They are also expected to interpret the capability and performance indices C_p, C_{pk}, P_p and P_{pk}.

7.8.1 Process Capability studies
Process stability
Before undertaking a process capability study, it is essential that the process is stable. Additionally we must know whether the process is producing normally distributed data. Green and Black Belts should therefore perform the following three analyses:

- Stability: The first test is to identify if any special causes are acting on the process. Is the process stable?
- Normality: The second test is to identify whether the process is producing normal data. Is the process normal?
- Capability: Finally it is then possible to determine if the process is capable. Is the process capable of meeting customer or business requirements?

Process capability versus Process performance
When reviewing process capability, two somewhat contrasting concepts need to be considered: 'Process Capability' and 'Process Performance'. Process capability shows what the process can do and process performance is what the process is actually doing. The gap between these two concepts can be seen as an opportunity for improvement.

Process capability is the potential of a process to produce products or services within the design specifications. These design specifications are called 'Lower Specification Limit' (LSL) and 'Upper Specification Limit' (USL). The difference between the USL and the LSL, is called the process tolerance. Process capability assumes only common cause variation and not special cause variation. Process capability represents the best performance of the process itself.

7

Process performance is defined as what the process is currently doing and is what the customer sees. Therefore, process performance is what typically concerns customers more than process capability. Process performance is based on the total variation of a process in the long term and assumes both common cause variation and special cause variation. Since a process is seldom perfectly stable, its Mean will drift in time and the standard deviation may vary in time too.

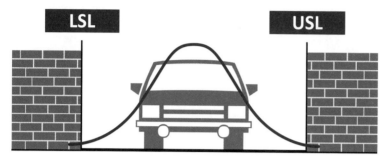

Figure 115 - *Process Capability*

In the Lean Six Sigma quality methodology, both process capability and process performance are reported to the organization as a 'Sigma level'. The higher the sigma level, the better the process is performing. A process capability analysis or process performance analysis can be done for the following purposes:

- To determine the baseline performance at the start of an improvement project.
- To demonstrate the improvements at the end of a project.
- To see the capability of a process to produce within specifications.
- To help product development select or change the process.
- To establish the interval between taking samples for process control.
- To define performance requirements for new equipment.
- To make choices between competing suppliers.

7

7.8.2 Process Capability indices

The 'Process Capability index' (C_p) has become the standard metric for defining what the process can do. The index C_p compares short-term process width to the maximum allowable variation as indicated by the tolerance. The index provides a metric of how well the process can satisfy the variability requirements if the process is perfectly stable. It does not take into account the location of the process. As already discussed in section 7.3, less process variation results in a higher quality level, which is equivalent to a higher C_p value. The index can be calculated using the following formula. In the formula the σ_{within} basically means that the σ is been calculated using data from a short period.

$$C_p = \frac{Specification\ width}{Process\ width} = \frac{USL - LSL}{6 \cdot \sigma_{within}}$$

The Motorola's 'Six Sigma approach' means that the process fits 2 times within the tolerance range. When centered, this equals a defect level of 0.0000002% (0.002 ppm; C_p = 2.0). Even today, many companies have capability indices C_p less than 0.67 for important parameters.

Let's assume four arbitrary processes are compared to the same specification requirements. The 'Lower Specification Limit' (LSL) of 10 and the 'Upper Specification Limit' (USL) of 30. Each of these four processes has a different standard deviation σ (respectively σ = 5.0, σ = 3.33, σ = 2.5 and σ = 1.67). The graph also shows the amount of defects that fall outside the specification. Note that the processes are centered.

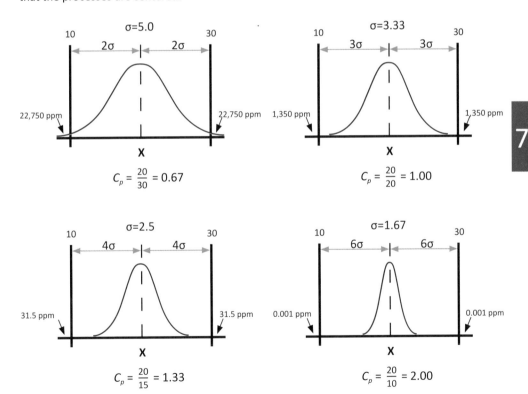

Figure 116 - Process Capability & Sigma levels

C_p is used as a basic introduction to the concept of process capability. Yet, it does not take into account any non-centering of the process relative to the specification limits of a parameter. The Process Capability index C_{pk} is defined as process capability, but corrected for non-centering. C_{pk} is a metric that takes into account both the spread and location. The index defines how close a process is running to its nearest specification limit, relative to the natural variability of the process. The larger the index, the higher the capability of the process to produce parts within the specification limits.

C_{pk} will always be less than or equal to C_p. C_{pk} will be equal to C_p only if the process is centered (Figure 230). C_{pk} and C_p should always be evaluated together, as a difference between C_p and C_{pk} indicates an opportunity for improvement by centering the process.

$$C_{pk} = \min (C_{pL}, C_{pU}), \text{ which is the lowest value of } C_{pL} = \frac{\bar{x} - LSL}{3 \cdot \sigma_{Within}} \text{ and } C_{pU} = \frac{USL - \bar{x}}{3 \cdot \sigma_{Within}}$$

It is important to realize that centering the process is much easier than reducing process spread. Centering the process normally requires an adjustment of one parameter, whereas reducing process spread often requires a more comprehensive design of experimental techniques.

The relation between specification width, sigma level, defect rate and process capability when the process is perfectly centered is demonstrated in Table 7.7.

Table 7.7. *Six Sigma metrics (centered process)*

Sigma level	Specification width	ppm outside spec	Percent defective	Cp; Cpk
1	2σ	317,311	31.7%	0.33
2	4σ	45,500	4.55%	0.67
3	6σ	2,700	0.27%	1.00
4	8σ	63	0.0063%	1.33
5	10σ	0.57	0.00006%	1.67
6	12σ	0.002	0.0000002%	2.00

7

7.8.3 Short-term and Long-term Capability

In the previous paragraph we mentioned that a centered 'Six Sigma Process' equals a defect rate of 0.002ppm. Those who have read other books about Six Sigma, might state that a Six Sigma performance equals a defect rate of 3.4ppm. So, what explains the difference? The reason is that in the past decades the initial mathematical Six Sigma philosophy has been adapted for process shifting and drifting over time. Many have adopted this paradigm of the 'Shifting $\bar{X}$ over time'.

Because of this, the overall variation (long-term variation) will be greater than the within variation (short-term variation). This is visualized in Figure 117.

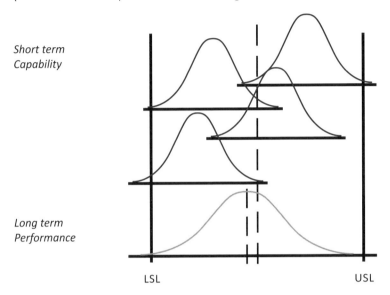

Figure 117 - *Short term Capability and Long term Performance*

It is clear that this amount of shift is not the same for all processes. In general a shift of 1.5σ shift is taken. Assuming a process has a tendency to drift towards 1.5σ over time. This means a distance between the $\bar{X}$ and the nearest specification limit of 4.5σ instead of 6.0σ. This is equivalent to a defect level of 3.4ppm at one side of the specification limits, as visualized in Figure 118. This is called a 'Six Sigma performance'.

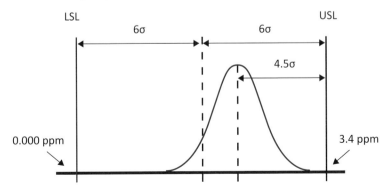

Figure 118 - *Six Sigma performance including 1.5 sigma shift*

7.8.4 Process Performance indices

Green and Black Belts should communicate clearly what data has been used for calculating process capability and process performance. If the analysis is based on common cause variation only, the Process capability indices (C_p and C_{pk}) should be used. If the analysis includes special cause variation or data over a longer period of time, Process Performance indices (P_p and P_{pk}) should be used.

The performance indices P_p and P_{pk} indices are very comparable to the capability indices C_p and C_{pk}. The P_p index compares the process performance to the maximum allowable variation as indicated by the tolerance. P_{pk} takes the process location as well as the process performance into account. The P_{pk} will always be less than or equal to P_p. P_{pk} will be equal to P_p only, if the process is centered.

The formulas are similar to the formulas of Process Capability. In the formula the $\sigma_{Overall}$ basically means that the σ is been calculated using data from a longer period.

$$P_p = \frac{USL - LSL}{6 \cdot \sigma_{Overall}}$$

$$P_{pk} = \min(P_{pL}, P_{pU}) \text{ , which is the lowest value of } P_{pL} = \frac{\bar{x} - LSL}{3 \cdot \sigma_{Overall}} \text{ and } P_{pU} = \frac{USL - \bar{x}}{3 \cdot \sigma_{Overall}}$$

The relation between specification width, sigma level, defect rate and process performance is demonstrated in Table 7.8:

Table 7.8. *Six Sigma metrics, incorporating 1.5σ shift*

Sigma level	Specification width	ppm outside spec	Percent defective	Ppk (long term)
1	2σ	691,462	69%	-0.17
2	4σ	308,538	31%	0.17
3	6σ	66,807	6.7%	0.50
4	8σ	6,210	0.62%	0.83
5	10σ	233	0.023%	1.17
6	12σ	3.4	0.00034%	1.50

The difference between Process Capability and Process Performance is demonstrated in Figure 119.

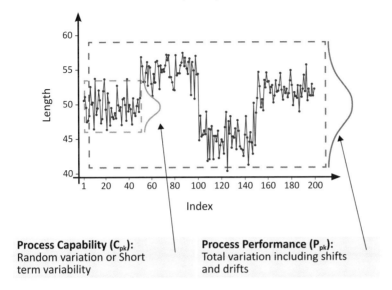

Process Capability (C$_{pk}$):
Random variation or Short
term variability

Process Performance (P$_{pk}$):
Total variation including shifts
and drifts

Figure 119 - *Process Capability versus Process Performance*

7

Improve

7.9 Design of Experiments (DOE)

'Design of Experiments' (DOE) includes the design and evaluation of experiments. DOE is a systematic and highly efficient way to conduct experiments, to examine the influence of factors and factor interactions on the responses. The DOE approach is based on the pioneering work of Sir Ronald Fisher, who applied DOE in agriculture in the early 1920s. He improved the productivity of British farms by using the Full Factorial method. For this great contribution he was knighted.

7.9.1 Principles of Experiments and terminology

Some 'Classic Problem Solver' experts will tell you to change only one factor at a time. The traditional 'One-Factor-At-a-Time' (OFAT) approach is inferior to DOE because OFAT experiments usually require more time consuming test runs and obtain only incomplete information regarding the process. OFAT does not reveal interactions between factors. Therefore OFAT is in inferior but still commonly used alternative for the more complicated 'Designed Experiments'.

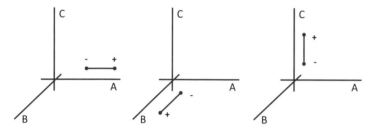

Figure 120 - *Changing one factor at a time (OFAT)*

7

Control

7.10 Statistical Process Control (SPC)

The objective of the Control phase is that solutions that have been implemented to improve the process performance will be embedded in the process and organization, to assure that improvements will sustain after the project has been closed. This is a critical element to make a Six Sigma project successful.

In the previous chapters we already explained a number of tools and techniques that can be used in the Control phase of a Six Sigma breakthrough project. All the techniques that we discussed in CIMM Level-I, II and III such as 5S, Standardized Work, Poka Yoke and the Control plan are very important for process control. In Figure 121 an overview is given of all the techniques that can be used in this phase. One important tool listed here has not been explained yet, which is 'Statistical Process Control' (SPC). This is an important tool to sustain improvements at both Level-IV and Level V.

Figure 121 - *Quality Control & Quality Assurance measures*

7

7.10.1 SPC Objectives and benefits

The concept of 'Statistical Process Control' (SPC) was introduced by Walter Shewhart in 1924 at Western Electric. Before that, products were tested and removed if defective. Shewhart used simple control charts for early detection of process variation. In the 1930's, SPC became popular in the UK and later in the United States. After World War II, Japan started the 'Quality revolution' and Deming taught them to use SPC to control and improve their processes.

*"Failure to use control charts to analyze data
is one of the best ways known to mankind
to increase costs, waste effort, and lower morale."*
Dr. Donald J. Wheeler

SPC helps to detect special cause variation. Special cause variation is variation that cannot be explained by common causes alone. Often this type of variation is very large when compared to common cause variation and is caused by problems that can be identified and often eliminated. SPC can be applied in different phases of a project and also at different maturity levels. SPC can be applied in the Define phase to identify new improvement opportunities. It can be applied in the Analyze phase to investigate the influence of certain factors on the response. SPC is also an important tool in the Control phase, at the end of an improvement project, to assure that results will be sustained.

A mistake that is often made by using SPC charts, is that the control limits on the SPC chart are used as specification limits. Although control limits and specification limits might look similar, there is a difference. Specification limits are set by the customer. Products outside these limits do not meet requirements and are not OK. Process Control limits however are calculated with the data from the process itself, normally based on a Capability study. Control limits are set in such a way that almost all of the process variation falls within these limits, but there is no relation to the specification limits. Knowing whether the process meets customer demands is extremely important indeed, but specification limits do not belong on a Control chart. If they are, the Control chart simply becomes an inspection tool and can no longer be considered a Control chart. The Control limits are normally set at +3 Sigma, which is equivalent to 99.73% of the data falling within the two Control limits.

7.10.2 Control charts

There are different SPC charts available. The chart you need to apply depends on the type of data that you want to analyze or control. Basically the following charts are most common:

- Xbar-R chart: for monitoring the means and ranges of subgroups of continuous data.
- I-MR chart: for monitoring individual data points and moving ranges for continuous data.
- P & NP chart: for monitoring defective items (Attribute data).
- C & U chart: for monitoring the number of defects per unit (Attribute data).

Yellow and Orange Belts are expected to understand and interpret the Xbar-R Chart, as this chart is the one mostly applied in statistical process control. The Xbar-R chart is used for monitoring process variation and for detecting the presence of special causes, by collecting subgroups from the process at regular intervals. The Xbar-R chart is used when at each of these intervals the subgroup size is small. Xbar can also be represented by $\bar{X}$ (an X with a bar over it).

The chart consists of two parts. The upper part of the chart represents the process mean. The lower part represents the process variation, approximated by the subgroup 'range'.

- 'Xbar' or $\bar{X}$ is the Mean of the measurements $x_1 .. x_i$ in the subgroup.
- 'Xbar-bar' or $\bar{\bar{X}}$ is the Mean of all 'Xbars'.
- 'R' is the Range of the measurements $x_1 .. x_i$ in the subgroup.

Example of an Xbar-R chart:

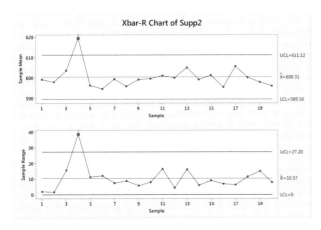

Figure 122 - *Xbar-R chart*

7

"If you keep your eye on the profit, you're going to skimp on the product. But if you focus on making really great products, then the profits will follow."

- Steve Jobs -

8
CIMM Process Level V
Creating sustainable processes

At the fifth level we will change from a reactive approach, where the focus was on improving the current situation, to a proactive approach, where we will focus on developing products that will meet customer expectations and will have no problems in production. This level is a combination of 'Product Lifecycle Management' (PLM) and 'Design for Six Sigma' (DfSS). Both PLM as DfSS describe a number of engineering development aspects from managing descriptions and properties through risk management, development and reliability. Design for Six Sigma is regularly applied by Black Belts, reliability engineers and in some cases by Green Belts. It requires knowledge about all tools and techniques that are explained in the sections about Level-I to IV.

8

8.1 Design for Six Sigma techniques

Most of the Lean and Six Sigma tools that have been explained in the first four CIMM Levels can also be applied in development and innovation projects. Applying these tools and techniques in the development process is called 'Design for Six Sigma' (DfSS) or 'Design for Lean Six Sigma'.

There are different roadmaps that are used in Design for Six Sigma. The most common roadmap used is the DMADV roadmap. DMADV is an abbreviation for Define, Measure, Analyze, Design and Verify. Both DMAIC and DMADV roadmaps are Six Sigma supporting roadmaps. While the DMAIC is applied in breakthrough projects (Level-III and IV), the DMADV is part of the Design for Six Sigma methodology and can be applied in problem prevention, development and innovation projects.

As DMADV projects very often start from a risk perspective, the project is very often initiated by an outcome of the Design FMEA. These projects are therefore called Risk Avoidance projects. A development project can have several risks that need to be investigated, so one development project might initiate several DMADV projects.

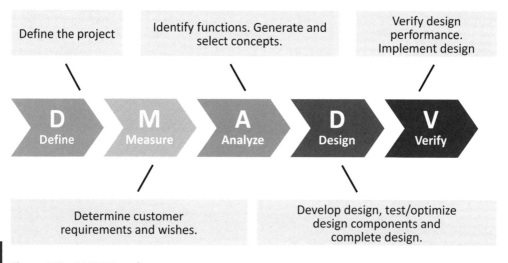

Figure 123 - *DMADV roadmap*

There are a number of similarities between the DMAIC and DMADV roadmaps. Both are data-driven approaches, they use similar tools and techniques and are used to drive defects to a minimum. To achieve this, both roadmaps use the same tools (e.g. MSA, Hypothesis testing, DOE). Therefore all tools and techniques that have been explained in Level-IV of this book, can also be applied in Level-V.

8

Appendix A
Yellow & Orange Belt certification

Within the domain of 'Continuous Improvement' individuals can be trained at four different levels. These levels are called Yellow Belt, Orange Belt, Green Belt and Black Belt.

Table A.1. *Overview of Belt levels*

Belt level	Level
Yellow Belt	Awareness
Orange Belt	Foundation
Green Belt	Practitioner
Black Belt	Expert

The LSSA - Lean Six Sigma Academy® was established in September 2009 with the objective to develop an international recognized certification scheme for all Lean Six Sigma Belt levels. The LSSA Exam Board has developed four syllabi with clear criteria for skills and competences. These syllabi specify which of the overall Lean Six Sigma tools and techniques are expected to be included within certain Belt level competencies. Lean Six Sigma training is provided by a global network of 'Accredited Training Organizations' (ATOs). These ATOs provide training programs that are aligned to the LSSA syllabi.

Examinations are provided through a number of 'Examination Institutes' (EIs), which use the syllabi to develop exams. The exams are open to all. Individuals can apply directly to the EIs or sign up via one of the ATOs. It is recommended that candidates receive training through an ATO to prepare for certification. Alternatively, candidates who wish to self-study have the option to apply directly to an EI for certification.

Examinations are provided through the following three Examination Institutes (EIs):

- APMG   APM Group Limited   www.apmg-international.com
- iSQI   International Software Quality Institute   www.isqi.org
- ECQA   European Certification and Qualification Ass.   www.ecqa.org

The structure of this book is based on the Lean Six Sigma Academy syllabi for Yellow Belts [6.] and Orange Belts [7.]. In order to prepare yourself for certification, we recommend you to review the LSSA syllabi and follow a training at a registered ATO.

Appendix B
References

[1.]   AIAG (2005). *Statistical Process Control (SPC), 2nd ed.* Southfield: Automotive Industry Action Group.

[2.]   Breyfogle, F.W. (2003). *Implementing Six Sigma: Smarter Solutions Using Statistical Methods, 2nd ed.* New York: Wiley.

[3.]   Imai, M. (1997). *Gemba Kaizen: A Common sense, Low-Cost Approach to Management.* New York: Mcgraw-Hill.

[4.]   Liker, J.K. (2004). *The Toyota Way: 14 Management Principles from the World's Greatest Manufacturer.* New York: McGraw-Hill.

[5.]   Rother, M., & Shook, J. (1999). *Learning to see: Value Stream Mapping to Add Value and Eliminate MUDA.* Cambridge: Lean Enterprise Institute, Inc.

[6.]   Theisens, H.C., & Meek, T. (2014). *Syllabus for Lean Six Sigma Yellow Belts 2nd ed.* Amstelveen: Lean Six Sigma Academy.

[7.]   Theisens, H.C., & Meek, T. (2014). *Syllabus for Lean Six Sigma Orange Belts 2nd ed.* Amstelveen: Lean Six Sigma Academy.

[8.]   Womack, J.P., & Jones, D.T. (1996). *Lean Thinking: Banish Waste and Create Wealth in Your Corporation.* New York: Simon & Schuster

Appendix C
Abbreviations

1PF	One-Piece-Flow
5S	5S-Housekeeping
5W	5-Why
6σ	Six Sigma
8D	Eight Disciplines
A3	A3-report
C&E Diagram	Cause and Effect Diagram
C&E Matrix	Cause and Effect Matrix
CI	Confidence Interval
CI	Continuous Improvement
CIMM	Continuous Improvement Maturity Model
CM	Change Management
COPQ	Cost of Poor Quality
Cp	Capability index
Cpk	Capability index
CTQ	Critical to Quality
DfSS	Design for Six Sigma
DfX	Design for Excellence
DMADV	Define, Measure, Analyze, Design, Verify
DMAIC	Define, Measure, Analyze, Improve, Control
DOE	Design of Experiments
DPM	Defects per Million
DPMO	Defects Per Million Opportunities
DPO	Defects Per Opportunity
DPU	Defects Per Unit
ERP	Enterprise Resource Planning
FIFO	First-In-First-Out
FMEA	Failure Mode and Effect Analysis
FTA	Fault Tree Analysis
G8D	Global 8D
GB	Green Belt
H_0	Null Hypothesis
H_A	Alternative Hypotheses
HOQ	House Of Quality
ICA	Interim Containment Action
IQR	Interquartile Range

JI	Job Instruction
JIT	Just-In-Time
JM	Job Methods
JR	Job Relation
KPI	Key Performance Indicator
KPIV	Key Process Input Variable
KPOV	Key Process Output Variable
LSL	Lower Specification Limit
LSS	Lean Six Sigma
LSSA	Lean Six Sigma Academy
MBB	Master Black Belt
MSA	Measurement System Analysis
OEE	Overall Equipment Effectiveness
OFAT	One-Factor-At-a-Time
Opex	Operational Excellence
OPL	One Point Lesson
OTD	On-Time Delivery
P	Probability
PCA	Permanent Corrective Actions
PDCA	Plan-Do-Check-Act Circle
PFD	Process Flow Diagram
PFM	Process Flow Map
PFMEA	Process Failure Mode, Effects, and Analysis
PM	Preventive Maintenance
Pp	Process Performance Index
Ppk	Process Performance Index
ppm	Parts per Million
Q	Quartile
QA	Quality Assurance
QC	Quality Control
QHSE	Quality, Health, Safety & Environment
QMS	Quality Management System
R&R% Study	Gage R&R Study
RCA	Root Cause Analysis
RPN	Risk Priority Number
S	Standard deviation of a dataset
s^2	Variance of a dataset
SCM	Supply Chain Management
SIM	Short Interval Management
SIPOC	Suppliers, Inputs, Process, Outputs, Customers
SMART	Specific Measurable Achievable Realistic Timely
SMED	Single Minute Exchange of Die
SOP	Standard Operating Procedure
SPC	Statistical Process Control
TOC	Theory of Constraints
SPL	Single Point Lesson
TPM	Total Productive Maintenance
TPS	Toyota Production System
TQM	Total Quality Management
USL	Upper Specification Limit

VOB	Voice Of Business
VOC	Voice Of Customer
VSM	Value Stream Map
WCM	World Class Manufacturing
WIP	Work in Progress
YB	Yellow Belt
Z	Z-Value
P	Correlation
σ	Sigma of a population
σ²	Variance in a population

Index